# Even the Rain

Written by Paul Laverty
Directed by Icíar Bollaín

**route**

First published in 2011 by Route
PO Box 167, Pontefract, WF8 4WW
info@route-online.com
www.route-online.com

© Screenplay: Paul Laverty

ISBN: 978-1-907862-05-2

Cover design:
GOLDEN
www.wearegolden.co.uk
From artwork supplied by Morena Films
www.morenafilms.com

Route support:
Guadalupe Balaguer Trelles, Ian Daley, Isabel Galán,
Juan Gordon, Emma Smith

*Even the Rain* English language version of the screenplay
for the Spanish language film *También la lluvia*

A catalogue for this book is available from the British Library

All rights reserved
No reproduction of this text without written permission

Printed by Lightning Source

# Contents

Paul Laverty — 7
*Screenwriter*

Icíar Bollaín — 21
*Director*

The Characters — 25

Even the Rain — 31
*Screenplay*

Cast and Crew — 157

*For Howard Zinn*

# Paul Laverty
*Screenwriter*

Around ten years ago, the brilliant historian Howard Zinn got in contact with me after seeing a film called *Bread and Roses*, directed by Ken Loach and written by myself. He wondered whether I might be interested in writing a script inspired by the spirit of the first chapter of his iconic book *A People's History of the United States*. I had a great passion for this book long before I met Howard and, in many ways, it was a dream come true to try and engage with a key moment in our history: the arrival of Columbus in the so-called New World. This is not the history of Columbus as the great discoverer, but instead it tells of what Columbus set in motion on his arrival among the Taino Indian population. The very first page of the book quotes from Columbus's own log: 'With fifty men we could subjugate them all and make them do whatever we want.' This first chapter, and indeed the whole book, is a homage to the resistance of ordinary people fighting those who have tried to subjugate them in different ways throughout history.

Howard wrote in his introduction: 'I don't want to invent victories for people's movements. But to think that history-writing must aim simply to recapitulate the failures that dominate the past is to make historians collaborators in an endless cycle of defeat. If history is to be creative, to anticipate a possible future without denying the past, it should, I believe, emphasize new possibilities by disclosing those hidden episodes of the past when, even in brief flashes, people showed their ability to resist, to join together, occasionally to win. I am supposing, or perhaps only hoping, that our future may be found in the past's fugitive moments of compassion rather than in its solid centuries of warfare. That, being as blunt as I can, is my approach to the history of the United States. The reader may as well know that before going on.'

Getting this film made has been a ten-year obsession, but the spirit of the above is what kept the effort alive during some very treacherous moments.

Howard helped enormously by sending me many of his own books for my research. It was a colossal effort to engage with the grand narrative and investigate what life was like five hundred years ago. To write a script, you don't just need to *know* what happened but you have to *smell* it; you need to get under each character's skin, and try to imagine what the world looked like from their point of view, whether it's a Taino child who first saw a bald and exhausted sailor land from Spain, or a young Catholic priest facing a furious congregation of colonists as he preached in favour of Indian rights. Howard at last gave me one terrific piece of advice, 'Stop reading. Start writing!'

I wrote the first versions as entirely period pieces, under the title *Are These Men?*, inspired by a question asked by a Dominican priest Padre Antonio Montesinos, who preached in March of 1511 in what was probably the first voice of conscience against the new Spanish empire. His denunciation of the mistreatment and murder of the indigenous population was passionate and brilliant: 'Look into an Indian's eyes. Are these not men? Do they not have rational souls? Are you not obliged to love them as yourselves?' Such dangerous opinions probably cost Montesinos his life.

The next stage was one familiar to many writers: the day of the double emails. I opened them in order. The first was a delighted one from Howard saying the project had been approved, and if I remember correctly was budgeted at around eighteen million dollars with casting just about to begin. The sweet adrenalin rush lasted all of thirty seconds. The second email was a brief note from a subdued Howard. He didn't understand the reasons, but the project had been cancelled.

Some characters don't give up very easily, and I have to say that this is true of Padre Antonio Montesinos. He may have died five hundred years ago, but he never gave me any peace. There was such raw power in his sermon delivered from that simple straw church that it kept forcing itself to the surface over the next few years in between all the other projects I was developing with my friend Ken Loach.

Despite the generosity of some readers I was never satisfied with the script *Are these Men?* and realised it needed a radical rethink, and not just a cosmetic rewrite. Ken too was a generous critic. We discussed the hazards of making a story set centuries ago come alive on the big screen. It is not like a novel where so much can be left to the imagination. In film, the devil is always in the detail, right in front of your eyes. Who would get their kit off to actually play the indigenous people of what became the Dominican Republic? Where would we shoot it? What language would they speak? What would they look like? Even for the Spaniards complex questions arose; how much has the Spanish language changed, and what would they sound like? There are significant barriers of credibility to jump, even before the daunting challenge of trying to penetrate the imaginary life of someone from the exterminated Taino population.

So I speculated on all sorts of weird and wonderful ways in which we might tell the historical story from a totally different perspective. One was actually set in the future and others used various framing devices – from day-dreaming, to teaching, to film-making and theatre – as a way of giving the story a present-day set of lenses. But I didn't want to jump into the daunting task of re-engaging with so much history, throwing out an entire script, and starting from scratch again, merely on spec, given that the project was very far from commercial. My friend Juan Gordon, a founding producer of Morena Films based in Madrid, decided to join the adventure.

I had the very good fortune to cross paths with the director Alejandro González Iñárritu. Alejandro was intrigued by the historical material too and, quite independently of my own critique, when he had read the period script he felt it should be told from a modern point of view and had many ideas. I felt very at home with his gut instinct.

However, a film about making films per se doesn't get the blood racing. It can be a useful framing device, and offers mischievous possibilities of constantly changing perspectives – actors can reject their characters' actions or words, and by implication set the audience on guard against our version of events in the film – but I always sensed we needed something contemporary and explosive, alongside the struggle of making a film, to echo against the past.

As I was doing the historical research it was stunning to see footage of the Water War on our TV screens. This popular insurrection in Cochabamba, Bolivia, came to a head in April of 2000. The riot scenes and confrontations were horrific. I couldn't help but notice how the indigenous population, armed with only sticks and stones once again, were now fighting a modern-day army. Dogs were set upon them once more. This time the dispute had nothing to do with gold, slavery or precious spices. It was a battle over water.

I wondered if we could mix these two realities separated by some five hundred years, and weave them together in a film shoot. Alejandro too was open to the notion. I was far from certain it would hold together, but it seemed to make sense to test the possibility. The only way to find out was to travel to Bolivia.

In May of 2005 I travelled to Cochabamba. It was a priority to speak to those who had participated in the Water War. I met Oscar Olivera who was President of the Cochabamba Federation of Factory workers and also the main spokesperson for the Coalition in Defence of Water and Life. The coalition was broadly based from many sectors of Bolivian life and was at the forefront of the battle against the multinational consortium – which included US corporation Bechtel – called Aguas del Tunari. The consortium in turn was backed forcefully by the Bolivian police and army.

Omar Fernandez, another grassroots leader, brought me to the countryside and introduced me to many peasants, both men and women, who also fought. An astonishing photograph of a young Indian woman with a sling-shot up against a line of soldiers will stick in my mind for ever. Abraham Grandyier walked me around the most marginal neighbourhoods of Cochabamba and he and his neighbours recalled in detail their stories of taking the main square during the riots. Fernando Salazar drove me to the mountains around the city and explained in fascinating detail how water had been used for centuries, by custom and practice, inside and outside the city. Students too shared their memories, along with coca growers whose assistance was key at the height of the struggle. It was sobering to see how crude and violent the privatisation process was, and how in one fell swoop it ignored generations of water use. Many citizens showed me where they had dug wells, and in one part of the town they showed the line of the trench they had dug which stretched seven kilometres into the distance behind a mountain where the community had bought a well. Deep down I reckon all these people suspected it took mild insanity on my part to try and mix their story with one from five hundred years ago, but I will never forget their amusement, patience and generosity as we marched around the dusty hills on the outskirts of Cochabamba.

The privatisation process, the Water War and aftermath are far too complex to go into in detail here, but anyone interested in finding out more would do well to read Oscar Olivera's eye-witness account called *¡Cochabamba! Water War in Bolivia*. But several key points attracted my attention. First, the IMF and World Bank put great pressure on what was seen as a Western-orientated Bolivian government to privatise the water supply. They even threatened to cut off other loans if they didn't comply. To implement the privatisation process the government passed Law 2029, which was so all-encompassing in its nature that it led many to believe that the multinational consortium would control water from every source. Oscar Olivera explains in his book how far the law went: 'The law also prohibited the peasants from constructing collection tanks to gather water from the rain. The rain, too, had been privatised. Law 2029 required people to ask for permission from the superintendent of water to collect the rain [...] furthermore, in deference to transnational corporations, it "dollarized" water payments. This didn't mean the people had to pay in US dollars, but if the boliviano (national currency) dropped in value against the dollar their water bill would increase to the equivalent price in US dollars.'

On the ground the consequences were brutal for the most vulnerable. Abraham and his colleagues told me the water rates were raised by around 35 per cent, which meant in practice paying 20 dollars per month for many who earned less than 70 dollars in a month. A man called Geoffrey Thorpe, the manager of the consortium, displaying all the sensitivity of a lamp-post, simply threatened to cut off their water supply if they didn't pay up. Oscar explained, 'The people look at water as something quite sacred. Water is a right for us, not something to be sold. The right to water is also tied to the traditional beliefs for rural people, as it has been since the time of the Incas. The traditional social practices and the ideas behind the use of water go beyond the distribution of water to encompass the idea that water belongs to the community and no one has the right to own the water.'

Water had become the new gold. Dogmatic theologians in soutanes from five hundred years ago now became dogmatic economists in suits. Both groups were equally certain of the One True Path, though it meant misery for the indigenous population. I recalled the first letter Columbus sent back to the Spanish Crown. It was really a sales document, pleading for more help. He waxed eloquently of the immense possibilities of 'souls for Christ' and 'great profit'. Now the mantra is 'privatisation' and 'great profit', the latter being guaranteed by contract between the Bolivian government and the consortium.

All these men and women, campesinos, cocaleros (coca workers), urban dwellers, trade unionists, students, and even the homeless children who decided to fight the police and the army knew they were risking their lives when they took to the streets and occupied the main square of Cochabamba. They were far from certain how the dispute would end and many feared a massacre. In fact, a couple of years later, in the Gas War of El Alto, the army moved in and shot dead around seventy protesters. Each and every person faced a dramatic choice, and I was struck by their understated courage.

The fact that the civilian population successfully managed to throw out a multinational consortium from the country, especially one backed by the might of police and army, was seen as a major victory against corporate power, and many Bolivians would argue that this gave the indigenous population greater confidence, which in turn gave massive impetus to the movement to later elect the first indigenous president in Bolivia, Evo Morales, who was involved in the Water War as leader of the cocaleros. The Water War reverberated throughout the whole continent as a massive blow against the neoliberal orthodoxy imposed on them from outside. Although they felt it was an outstanding victory they were under no illusions that the most difficult challenge was to come: to find finance from alternative sources to implement the gargantuan task of providing clean water to all, under public control in an impoverished country exploited for centuries. And so it proved to be. In life there are seldom clear-cut black-and-white victories.

It was clear the Water War was massively significant on many levels. But how the hell was I going to combine all this with Columbus, Bartolomé de las Casas and the Indian rebel Hatuey? Would it just seem totally outlandish? In this new version Howard was no longer involved, though we exchanged many friendly emails. On my return I wrote the first draft of a totally new screenplay trying to interweave the two time zones in and around two fictional characters, Sebastián, an idealist director, and the cynical opportunist producer, Costa. Over the next two years or so I met Alejandro on many occasions as we wrestled with the material in between our other projects. Alejandro was a terrific collaborator, full of great insight, and with a brilliant visual imagination. He was a very generous collaborator too, and I will always be very grateful for his significant contribution and his friendship. In the great gamble freelancers make with their time, the mere possibility and hope of getting a huge project off the ground is vital to provide the energy to keep fighting for a better story. It is also fair to say we had different inclinations about the DNA of the story, and we both, on the very best of terms, decided to go our own separate ways. Alejandro went to Barcelona to make *Biutiful*, and I joined up with Ken Loach to make *Looking for Eric* and *Route Irish*.

Again, Padre Antonio Montesinos, from five hundred years back, and Juan Gordon, from around the corner, refused to let this story slip from view. And then something very unexpected happened. My partner Icíar Bollaín had followed the ups and downs of this odyssey with great patience, for so long in fact that our oldest son Lucas, now ten, was a baby when I first started talking to Howard Zinn. Out of the blue she said she would consider directing the story if we were up for it. Me and Icíar had always speculated that bringing up our three boys was a big enough challenge without the gamble of making a film together. But I was delighted at the prospect, and convinced that she would have the talent and energy to pull it off.

The script at that stage was a strange beast, and a dangerous one for a director. It had an intricate, or perhaps just a messy, structure. There were many dense and meaty scenes from the period piece, the Water War too was highly complex (the challenge was always to convey its essence, with the rest suggested under the surface like an iceberg) and yet we needed time for the fictional characters to live and breathe in what would be the heart of the story: the unfolding of the shoot of the period film. There were many conundrums... how talented, for example, were the fictional film-makers, and what was their sensibility? How should we shoot period, contemporary, and 'making of' scenes? Would there be a stylistic difference or should we try to knit these strands together as one? Icíar too took a leap of faith, because on paper it was very difficult to judge whether the period and modern scenes would weave together or not; there was every possibility the juxtaposition might look ridiculous, or worse, heavy-handed. In addition she foresaw how difficult it would be to shoot in the tropics, to say nothing of recreating riot scenes in the middle of a city with a modest budget and tight schedule. But she had the bottle and dived in to the adventure.

Juan Gordon as producer faced dangerous waters; not only did he have a strange script to promote, but it coincided with the financial crisis which meant that raising finance for projects off the beaten track became much more difficult. I have surreal memories of Icíar and Juan running from one meeting to another at Cannes in 2009 with lots of nice words ringing in their ears, but not much cash jingling in their pockets. Icíar was massively practical; she simplified many script contortions, and was extremely shrewd about how to tackle the vital question of casting – how to get a modern-day indigenous community to play the Tainos from the time of Columbus.

I suspect that few outside the film-making community realise how fine the line is between failure and success. It was an incredibly complex package to put together, and as the summer of 2009 ticked on we realised time was running out again on another year, and that Juan would have to green-light the shoot immediately if we were not to be caught by the rainy season in the jungles of Bolivia. It was now time for Juan to take a leap, and he did, showing considerable courage since not everything had been finalised. Sometimes film-making is one big gamble, and the pressures on producers greatly underestimated.

Others will talk about the shoot itself, but my lasting memory will be visiting hundreds of extras in the jungle near Villa Tunari, with lines of vehicles sliding about in the mud as the rain thundered down. The following day, against expectation, Padre Antonio Montesinos organised good weather for us to carry out the grand execution of poor old rebel Hatuey. Many of the Spanish extras were on the point of fainting as their chain armour was sprayed with water to stop them melting in the suffocating heat while others were treated for an endless array of insect bites. To top it all, wardrobe staff faced an armed hold-up in their hotel. In truth, we had a marvellous cast and crew and I am immensely grateful to every one of them.

Costa, the fictional opportunist producer in the film, exploited the indigenous communities by paying them two dollars a day. Displaying crude cynicism and complete lack of professional integrity, a minority of reviewers in the US, without any evidence whatsoever, assumed we had done the same. For the record, our producers in the real shoot did not. Many of the same grass-roots organisations I met four years previously in preparation for the screenplay helped us out once again when we came to make the film. The production team, in negotiation with the organisations, agreed what was considered to be a fair wage for a day's work for each extra, and in addition, so that the community benefitted beyond those fortunate enough to work, an extra payment was made to the corresponding community. So for example in one place they wanted bricks to build a school. In another place they wanted computers. With the water organisation in Cochabamba it was agreed to make a contribution of 30,000 euros to help pay for a water truck, supplemented by another 10,000 euros which was awarded to Iciar as a prize from AECID, the Spanish Agency for International Development Cooperation. It was also a great source of joy for me to meet so many extras on set who had actually risked life and limb in the Water War and were now working with us, with great enthusiasm, to recreate it on film.

On 27 January 2010, while we were editing the film, Howard Zinn, after a lifetime of teaching, writing and activism, died while swimming at the age of eighty-seven. It was a blow to lose such a wonderful collaborator, and modest friend, and I wish we could have sat in that darkened cinema together, along with another thousand strangers at the Toronto Film Festival, to watch the first public screening, and afterwards for him to have participated in what was a wonderful debate. It was not to be, but I was massively touched by the spontaneous applause from the audience when his name appeared on screen.

Howard's books are a homage to the courage and creativity of ordinary people. He doesn't romanticise them, but he makes them central to our understanding. Despite its deficiencies I hope our film is a modest contribution in the same vein. As I write these few lines now, and at the same time watch the TV screens beam mass resistance to one dictatorship after another throughout the Middle East and North Africa, my mind is flooded with the faces and words of those who took to the streets of Cochabamba a decade ago. It never ceases to amaze how much they pay for basic human rights. It seems appropriate to leave the last word to Howard. 'Not to believe in the possibility of change is to forget that things have changed, not enough of course, but enough to show what is possible. We have been surprised before in history. Indeed, we can do the surprising.'

**Icíar Bollaín**

*Director*

Directing Paul's script presented an enormous and exciting challenge: to make three movies in one. Firstly, a period drama, secondly, the near-contemporary story of the water conflict and, finally, a film connecting the shoot itself and the personal journeys of the main characters, Sebastián and Costa, and the decisions they are forced to make. Maintaining the tension and drama within and between each of these three stories and leading the audience from one to the other was the greatest challenge. But in truth this complexity was a gift – a director is rarely given such an original story, so complex and with such compelling and multilayered characters, and one that resonates so richly with one of the most crucial conflicts of this century.

Given the complexity of the script, it was a priority to highlight Costa's personal journey, his evolution and his relationship with Daniel, played by the Bolivian Juan Carlos Aduviri, the character who most directly affects him. During the shoot and the editing, I always tried to find those moments that showed this evolution – sometimes nothing more than a look, a moment of loneliness, a silence. I felt very clearly from the outset that the movie's emotional heart (and power) would arise from the conflict of these two prominent characters and from Costa's developing perception of Daniel's reality: a reality much harsher, much harder than his own.

Although I had already worked with non-professional actors, the challenge here was one of scale. Not two or three non-professionals, but twenty or thirty, with some cast as protagonists not extras. For me, the effort was fully rewarded: when the casting is good, the performances possess a great truth, they turn out to be very touching and truly authentic. And when you add generous professionals like Gael, Luis and Karra, the results are very convincing. I have to say the Bolivian extras were impressive. They performed wonderfully and as many times as necessary, with an unflagging enthusiasm without which the film wouldn't have half the life it has.

All in all, *Even the Rain* is by far the most complicated movie I have made. It has been an adventure and a great challenge for everyone involved, but very exciting. How do you eat an elephant? Bite by bite, as the saying goes. How do you shoot a movie with so many extras, characters, and so much action? Shot by shot. That's how I faced it, planning every scene meticulously, casting and directing all the extras individually, working phrase by phrase with actors who had never acted before, and relying on a remarkable cast and crew, Spanish as well as Bolivian.

## The Characters

COSTA
When Costa lands in Bolivia to produce a film he has no idea how the experience will affect him personally or how much it will change him before he leaves.

Pragmatic and cynical, he has no problem paying people poorly (if at all) or shooting in locations that are historically inaccurate as long as he gets his film made. The Indians 'look all the same' to him until he clashes with indigenous leader Daniel. And he doesn't care about the whole 'water thing' either… until it blows up in his face.

His friendship and loyalty to Sebastián and the film lead him to bribe anybody he has to, but also to sell out and betray… and finally to choose between helping his friend with the film and helping a desperate mother in a desperate fight.

SEBASTIAN
More tolerant and apparently more humane than Costa, Sebastián tries to overturn the myths we've been told by historians and filmmakers in the past. Passionate and melancholic, he becomes obsessed with finishing his film, no matter what, despite the delicate social context faced by hundreds of indigenous Indians participating in the shoot being paid a couple of dollars a day. 'This conflict will end and it will be forgotten… Our film won't be.' Sebastián fights with ideas, not stones. He's determined to expose an injustice that took place five hundred years ago, even if that means turning his back on an injustice taking place right in front of him.

## DANIEL

Bolivian and with strong indigenous features, he is a born leader who can't be tamed. Sebastián finds him fascinating and gives him an important part: Hatuey, the rebel leader who rose up against the Spanish conquistadores.

Costa says he 'stinks of trouble'. But despite Costa's objections, Daniel plays his part with enormous strength and charisma, until the water conflict becomes his priority.

For Costa and Sebastián, life is making movies; for Daniel, life is staying alive. Costa and Sebastián are fighting to get their film finished; Daniel is fighting for something as basic and vital as drinking water. Costa and Sebastián risk their money and prestige. Daniel and many others like him risk their lives.

## ANTON

Provocative, brilliant, educated and tremendously unhappy, the Spanish actor playing Columbus is a loner, a drinker, bitter and funny, probably sick... and incredibly talented. He plays Columbus – which could be the last role of his life – with the same passion with which he questions him. Anton is a cynic, but he turns out to be the most coherent and humane when the conflict breaks out around them.

## ALBERTO

Alberto is another passionate actor who plays the radical figure Bartolomé de las Casas with intensity. Like Anton, he has studied his character in depth; but unlike Anton, and contrary to what the real Bartolomé would probably have done, when things get out of hand, he scampers and leaves the film. Ironically, the good Alberto, playing the father of human rights, the man who stood up to a whole empire in defence of the Indians, who denounced the greed and cruelty of the conquistadores, is a terrified man in the face of real violence.

*JUAN*

Playing the role of Antonio Montesinos, Juan is an actor who goes 'less by the book' than the others. Once again, the actor and character represent a contrast. The radical and charismatic priest who defended the Indians in 1511 is played a young actor who is always joking and messing around. He's anything but 'intense'.

But even out of costume and in rehearsal, on an unfinished set, he manages to make the words of the Dominican's famous sermon of 1511 vibrate with strength and modern relevance.

# Even the Rain
*Screenplay*

*Note on English version of the script*

The screenplay was chopped and changed many times before the final shoot, which of course was filmed in Spanish and Quechua. This present English version contains some scenes that were shot, but cut from the final film, but these scenes will appear in the DVD as extras. It also contains parts of scenes that were cut in the weeks running up to the shoot, and were never filmed.

The biggest change between this screenplay and the final film relates to two Bolivian characters called Daniel and Enrique. Daniel was envisaged as an ex-military figure who became a bodyguard to a grass-roots community leader, Enrique, in Cochabamba. It was a very difficult casting process in Bolivia, but after we had the good fortune to find Juan Carlos Aduviri, who had never acted before, we decided to merge the two characters of Daniel and Enrique into one, as was originally the case in an older version of the script. We changed the dialogue to fit Juan Carlos, who played the new community leader Daniel and historical Indian rebel Hatuey, while Enrique disappeared into the sunset.

We decided to cut all reference to Sebastián's girlfriend Rose.

In the course of editing the film, following the sharp observations of editor Ángel Hernández Zoido, we decided to place some moments of the water dispute earlier in the story.

1.VALLEY OF COCHABAMBA, BOLIVIA – DAY

A familiar shudder and deep vibrations.

SKY: A quite stunning sight; with high range mountains in the background, a huge transport helicopter hauls an enormous cross, some thirty feet high, over the valley of Cochabamba.

The words **BOLIVIA, 2000**, appear at the bottom of the screen.

HOUSES AND DUSTY STREETS (in a marginal barrio): Children run from humble shacks made of corrugated iron, rough breeze block and adobe. They are beside themselves with excitement as they stare up at the sky.

The helicopter now swoops over the children who are gathered round a community well filling buckets with water. The children point up at the sky, shouting and laughing.

Over this image, the TITLE OF THE FILM

**EVEN THE RAIN**

The cross and helicopter disappear into the distance.

The OPENING CREDITS roll over the images of the cross and typical rural life scenery [people watering crops, water flowing through streams], meshed into:

2. EXT. BARRIO ON THE OUTSKIRTS OF THE CITY.
MAKESHIFT CASTING OFFICE, COCHABAMBA – DAY

A scene of some chaos as hundreds of Indians, men and women, old and young, form a long queue which stretches from inside the building where the casting is taking place, and for some 100 metres along the street and then around the block. [Many hold a leaflet advertising an open casting session.]

Now a rougher film texture, a camera manned by a less steady hand... Indian faces; their weather-beaten hands; their feet, often protected by little more than sandals. A girl, MARIA, is recording images for the 'Making Of', with a small video camera.

Two casting assistants, a man and a woman – one, with a mobile phone, at the beginning of the queue and another at the end – are literally swept off their feet. Four hefty security guards are on the point of being overwhelmed by the crowd and their patience wears thin.

Two men come out of the small building: COSTA [producer, late thirties, strongly built; behind his tough, coarse demeanour, intelligent eyes] and SEBASTIAN [writer/director, early thirties – talented, cerebral, headstrong, totally driven and single minded; a strange mixture of steely strength and delicate fragility]. A girl, ROSE, Sebastián's girlfriend, young and bright, walks behind them, closely observing. [Sebastián and Rose speak English to each other throughout.] Costa and Sebastián view the queue with growing alarm as they approach the production assistant.

> SEBASTIAN
> Christ... there's hundreds... and lots more still coming... look!

> COSTA
> Open fucking session, Sebastián! I told you this might happen! [To the assistant]... Tell them no more... not one more!

> SEBASTIAN
> We can't do that...

> COSTA
> We can't see them all! [To Sebastián] Pick the ones you like and get the rest out of here...

Sebastián doesn't move as he studies the chaos with a heavy heart.

COSTA (CONT'D)
Come on! Get a move on… Pick them out!

Sebastián, with the casting assistant and Maria, who's still taking her 'Making Of' footage, walks along the queue. Sebastián, embarrassed, can barely look them in the eye as he contemplates worried faces desperate for work. A few are very old and doubled up with age; passing them is even more painful for him.

Sebastián picks out faces on impulse. The 'Making Of' camera passes slowly over their faces, homing in on their Indian features. The luckier ones enter the building while the production assistant informs the others they have to go. Humiliation and disappointment all round.

Suddenly a scuffle begins: shouts are heard further down the queue as two people join friends who are already in the queue. Sebastián and Costa look to see what's going on.

DANIEL [a physically intimidating Indian, late thirties] with his twelve-year-old daughter, BELEN, by his side, confront a stressed-out CASTING WOMAN and a burly security GUARD who is Indian. The casting woman speaks 'Spanish' Spanish [ie from Spain]. Some of those in the queue speak 'Quechuañol', a mixture of Bolivian Spanish and Quechua. They don't understand each other.

CASTING WOMAN
I'm sorry! No more!… Far too many… We can't see you all…

A Bolivian production ASSISTANT repeats the instructions in Quechua for those who don't understand what is going on.

DANIEL
Yes you can… We've waited hours…

CASTING WOMAN
You have to go…

DANIEL
No we don't.

From the queue, several shout out in agreement. More tension.

The guard grabs Daniel by the arm and tries to pull him out of the queue.

> GUARD
> [In Quechua] You heard the girl... on your way...

> DANIEL
> [Calm] Let go of my arm...

> GUARD
> Fuck off smart ass or I'll break your neck.

The guard pulls harder.

In a flash Daniel has the guard face down on the ground, arm twisted up his back. The horrified assistant screams out. Two other security guards rush towards Daniel, with Sebastián and Costa in hot pursuit.

> ASSISTANT
> [Shouting] Stop it! Enough!

It stops them all. Sebastián stares at Daniel.

> SEBASTIAN
> It's okay... everyone calm down... please let go of him.

Daniel, his knee still in the guard's back, pulls out a leaflet out of his back packet.

> DANIEL
> 'Everyone gets a chance,' it says. [Pointing to Belen] She wants hers...

> BELEN
> I want to be an actress...

Sebastián stares at Daniel in fascination as he releases the guard. Both man and child hold his eye. Belen takes her father's hand. There is a strength to them both.

COSTA
[Half to himself] Fuck... that's all we need... [To the crowd]... I'm sorry... we can't see you all... you'll have to go...

DANIEL
[Holding up the leaflet] We're not going anywhere!

Costa looks round at the large crowd now supporting Daniel. He goes over to Sebastián and whispers quietly.

COSTA
Get rid of him... I don't care how... this guy's trouble... tell him you'll have a look at the girl later...

Sebastián says nothing; he just looks at Costa for a second, then at Daniel.

SEBASTIAN
[To Daniel] You're right... [to Costa and Assistant] We'll see everyone... however long it takes...

Belen looks at her father in triumph as the casting assistant glances nervously at Costa. A moment between Sebastián and Costa as the latter shakes his head.

SEBASTIAN (CONT'D)
[To Assistant, nodding at Daniel] This guy's got something... make sure you record him as well.

The assistant nods and then tries to calm others in the queue.

COSTA
[Resigned] Let's get a move on... They're waiting for us...

They head towards a 4 x 4.

COSTA (CONT'D)
Fucking hell Sebastián.

A sudden deafening sound. The helicopter and dangling cross sweep above them. Shouts, jokes, laughter and fascination from the Indians in the queue as the strange sight disappears into the distance.

                    COSTA (CONT'D)
        Move it!

3. INT. 4 X 4, COUNTRYSIDE – DAY

The 4 x 4 speeds through the Bolivian countryside. Costa drives like a man possessed on a terrible road. Sebastián is seated beside Rose and Maria.

[After tension above, now an atmosphere of irreverence. Despite Costa's cringing political incorrectness he still makes Sebastián smile; sense of deep personal affinity between them despite their differences. Maria is sharp and mischievous.]

                    MARIA
        Costa! Slow down you lunatic!

She points the camera at him.

                    MARIA (CONT'D)
        Where are we going?

                    COSTA
        To meet Jesus Christ!

Maria swings the camera round to Sebastián.

                    MARIA (MAKING OF)
        Tell me... here we are in Bolivia... doesn't make
        much sense...

Sebastián nods and with sense of embarrassment he rolls his eyes.

                    MARIA (CONT'D)
        Landlocked... twenty thousand feet up the
        Andes... thousands of miles from the
        Caribbean... it's mad...

### SEBASTIAN
[Indicating Costa] Arsehole there thinks Columbus came by parachute…

### COSTA
Never mind that… It's full of hungry Indians! 'Extras'… thousands of the bastards! None of that digital shit… I want some scale… a bang for our bucks!

### SEBASTIAN
[Serious] So fucking sloppy… Have you seen what they look like? They're Quechuas!

### COSTA
[At a loss] So?

### SEBASTIAN
From the Andes! What the fuck has Columbus got to do with Indians from the Andes?

### COSTA
From the Andes or the Pandes! Who gives a fuck? They're Indians… that's what you bloody wanted…

Sebastián shakes his head.

### COSTA (CONT'D)
Don't be so fucking choosy… they all look just the same…

### ROSE
Costa!

### SEBASTIAN
Jesus Christ! Can you imagine an English-speaking film with Eskimos playing New Yorkers? That's what it's like!

### COSTA
Brains up your ass… too many fucking European films festivals man… [To camera]… Look, we can

do good business here... Transport, security, hotels, catering... anything you want... it's all here. I did five different budgets... five different countries... this came out top by a mile...

MARIA
So it's all about money then?

SEBASTIAN
[Nodding] It's always about money... or lack of money... [indicating Costa, taking the piss] or cheapskate fucking producers with no taste cutting corners...

COSTA
We could have done this in English! Got twice the budget! Twice the audience... I had the deal almost done... till you fucked up!

SEBASTIAN
Spaniards spoke Spanish cabrón! What does that say about us if we do it in English?

COSTA
Says we're fucking smart...

SEBASTIAN
Selling out! The whole project unravels from the first fucking syllable in a false language! What will they think in Latin America?

COSTA
Don't tell me... I'll never sleep again.

Rose can't help but laugh.

SEBASTIAN
[Serious] We're up against it... no stars, no sex... no special effects... [His frustration and anger breaks through] Just seventy million dead Indians!... Ten times more than the holocaust and they look at me as if I'm making it up...

                         MARIA
    And did you?

Sebastián stares silently at the camera for a brief second, then smiles.

A deafening roar above their head. Costa lets out a cowboy yell as the low-flying helicopter with dangling cross not far above their heads sweeps over them.

                         COSTA
    Fuck me Seb... look at that!

Costa leans back and both he and Sebastián grab each other's hands.

                     COSTA (CONT'D)
    We're going to get through this... I fucking
    promise you!

Costa swerves off the road and onto a tiny little track and charges along at speed over the bumps as they all shout and joke amidst the excitement.

4 EXT. COUNTRYSIDE. CLEARING – DAY

Costa is in full flight as Sebastián, close by, looks on with growing anxiety. Rose is at his side. Maria captures some of this on her video.

In one hand Costa has a mobile phone to be in contact with the helicopter; in the other, a megaphone, to instruct the labourers waiting below for the cross. The cross sways dangerously and the noise of the helicopter is deafening.

                         COSTA
    [Shouting] Easy now... slow down! Slow down!
    It's swinging! Grab the fucking thing... tell them
    to grab it! Now! Do they understand fucking
    Spanish?

                       SEBASTIAN
    [To Costa] Christ... far too dangerous...

43

                    COSTA
[Ignoring him, to the pilot] Down... slowly...
easy... down again...

The cross swings dangerously.

                  SEBASTIAN
Get them out of there!

                    COSTA
Easy... easy boys... you're doing fine...

                  SEBASTIAN
I can't stand this...

Rose, nervous too, is transfixed by the manoeuvre. Half a dozen Indians grab the bottom of the cross as the tail-end is laid on the ground. Gradually the cross is laid flat as the helicopter blades blow strong gusts of wind around the men. The top end of the cross descends gradually as Costa loudly exhorts the crew.

                    COSTA
Easy... doing fine boys...

Suddenly, with just some nine feet to go, the hook snaps and the top end of the cross crashes to the ground, narrowly missing several Indians who jump back in horror.

                  SEBASTIAN
Fuck!

Shouts and curses in Quechua. Nervous laughter too.

                    COSTA
Everybody okay?

No casualties. Relief all round. Some jokes and nervous smiles after the scare.

                COSTA (CONT'D)
[To camera] Now for my next trick...

                           SEBASTIAN
            Fucking hell Costa! Should have had
            professionals… And a crane!

                             COSTA
            Yeah… know how much we just saved?…
            Thirty-five grand! Calm down… we made it.

Costa moves over and claps a few Indians on the back.

                         COSTA (CONT'D)
            Great work boys! Let's go… beers are on me!

A charming wink at camera from Costa before he heads off.

The 'Making Of' camera turns to Sebastián…

                           SEBASTIAN
            [Snapping] Turn that off!

Maria obeys. She watches Sebastián, still anguished, move over and look down quietly at the enormous prostrate cross. He stares at it for a long moment. Rose joins him and takes his arm.

                       SEBASTIAN (CONT'D)
            [In English] Hope to hell I get through this…

                             ROSE
            [English] I know you will.

## 5. EXT. GARDENS OF A FIVE-STAR HOTEL, BOLIVIA – DAY

A preliminary 'reading' of the script within the privileged confines of the beautiful gardens. Sebastián, accompanied by his assistant, with Costa lurking in the background, sit with some dozen or so Spanish ACTORS, playing the sailors who first arrived with Columbus.

[Generally we see Sebastián come to life as he directs. He's sharp, aware, and lives the action taking place in front of his eyes. He takes delight in the process and his talent shows. He's generous and sensitive with the actors.]

ANTON, the actor playing COLUMBUS, grabs a sizeable glass of wine and gulps it down. Sebastián studies him with some concern. [Anton has a real 'lived in' face; a man that has tasted everything life has to offer. Something big, maverick, unpredictable, sharp, but ultimately humane behind his dark eyes.]

### SEBASTIAN
[To Assistant] Is he pissed already?

The assistant shrugs her shoulders as they watch Anton rumble over towards his seat with the script dangling lazily in his hand.

Near the group, THREE BOLIVIAN WAITERS [number 3 is a woman] by a table laden with drinks, snacks and exotic fruit to which the actors help themselves. Throughout the scene, waiters 1 and 2 struggle to suppress their growing hilarity, while waitress number 3 is more restrained.

Anton nods regally at Sebastián as he clumsily takes his seat. Two young actors, ALBERTO and JUAN, also study his every movement, from a slight distance. Sebastián gives the assistant the thumbs up to start.

### ASSISTANT
[Reading description from script] Stunned faces of three Taino children hiding in the branches... From their point of view we see Columbus and his men take their first steps in the 'New World'. Several small boats have been pulled up on the water's edge. A disgusting smell pervades the air as strange bedraggled creatures, [the waiters smile at the description] some bearded, some bald, trip and stumble their way towards them over the sand... The youngsters in the trees struggle to make sense of the strangers below them...

### ANTON/COLUMBUS
[With stunning energy and immense power] I, Christopher Columbus, in the name of Jesus Christ, Son of the One True God, humble servant of King Ferdinand of Aragon and Queen

> Isabella of Castile, do hereby take possession of
> all these lands and seas and all they contain...

Anton jumps up and grabs an umbrella from a table by an astonished waiter, drops to his knees and stabs the umbrella into the middle of the lawn as if it were the royal banner of Ferdinand and Isabella.

> COLUMBUS
> ...and do hereby claim sovereignty over said lands
> and seas on behalf of Their most gracious
> Majesties...

Waiters 1 and 2 view this with some amusement, but try not to show it.

> COLUMBUS (CONT'D)
> Let us give thanks to the Virgin Mother for this
> great triumph and for delivering us unto safety...

The other 'sailors' drop to their knees and say a 'Hail Mary, full of grace'. Waiters 1 and 2, like kids in a church, have trouble controlling their giggles as the prayer continues.

The actors, led by Columbus, walk around the lawn as if examining the very first settlement they ever set eyes on in the New World.

[On impulse, Columbus, followed by the others, begins to 'use' the waiters behind the table as impromptu props for rehearsal.]

The waiters almost stand to attention and don't know how to react to the scene being played out before them. The actors move closer, scrutinising them.

> COLUMBUS (CONT'D)
> [To his CAPTAIN and NOTARY] They've never
> seen a horse... ever.

Columbus surveys his imaginary village then looks up at the surrounding hills.

COLUMBUS (CONT'D)
[Glancing at hotel] That must be their village up there... Thank God they are peaceful...

The waiters glance at each other. Waitress number 3 is beginning to feel very embarrassed.

CAPTAIN
Good place for a fort...

COLUMBUS
Mingle with them... there will be a reward for the first man who finds gold... treat them well... [grabbing a delicate pastry]... we need their food...

Just as they are about to disperse, Columbus grabs the Captain by the arm.

COLUMBUS (CONT'D)
Find out what weapons they have...

Eyes of waitress 3 flash at them in bewilderment as they are studied at deeply uncomfortable close quarters by the actors.

NOTARY
Admiral!... Quick!... You must see this!

They rush over to surround and inspect the abashed woman. She is wearing a gold earring with a modern design. [Again, Sebastián's eyes shine. He steps closer, engaged by the action.]

Columbus stares at her for a long moment. He gets carried away; he stretches out his arm and grabs the waitress's ear lobe. He pretends to undo the earring as the waitress's eyes flash. Columbus examines the imaginary piece in his hand.

Columbus and the Captain turn to look at each other. They are both visibly moved. [A quiet nod from Sebastián who appreciates their skill.]

COLUMBUS
[Whisper] Gold...

The word filters through from one man to the next like a sacred whisper.

> VOICES
> Gold... gold... gold... gold... gold...

The men crowd around the stunned waitress. Columbus stands before her and stares into her eyes.

> COLUMBUS
> Where is the gold?

The waitress freezes.

> COLUMBUS (CONT'D)
> [Stronger, with overwhelming power] Gold!
> Where is the gold? You know what I mean,
> woman... [grabbing her other earring] this...
> Gold!

The waitress's eyes dart around her in rising distress.

> COLUMBUS (CONT'D)
> [Now way over the top, bellowing like a
> wounded animal] Never mind the fucking
> gold... I need a drink!

Sebastián chuckles [he gives the thumbs up to Costa] and the rest laugh openly as the rehearsal breaks up.

Anton/Columbus approaches the sullen waitress.

> ANTON/COLUMBUS (CONT'D)
> My apologies... Actors... selfish to the very core.

Columbus helps himself to two glasses of wine. One he downs in one gulp, and then approaches Sebastián with the other in his hand.

> SEBASTIAN
> Terrific Anton... we'll do this scene at the end
> by the coast...

Alberto and Juan approach.

ANTON
Ah… here they come… Our two radical
priests… Bartolomé de las Casas and Antonio
Montesinos… Been polishing up your little halos
have we? Feel devout inside?

The two young actors don't know how to take him. An embarrassed moment between them.

ALBERTO
[To Sebastián] Found your rebel Hatuey yet?

SEBASTIAN
Seen lots of actors… [shaking his head]… I want
a real Indian…

Anton guffaws. They can sense real bite and contempt.

ANTON
Can hardly be precious about the detail! Here we
are in fucking Bolivia! [Looking Sebastián in the
eye] What a dumb idea…

He downs the second glass of wine.

ANTON (CONT'D)
All we need now is [flicking up his hands at
speed as if drawing pistols from a holster] Butch
Cassidy and Sundance!

He's just about to walk off but stops to confront Sebastián again.

ANTON (CONT'D)
[Scoffing] Just for your information the entire
Taino population which greeted Mr Columbus
was fucking wiped out… as dead as the dodo!…
A real Indian my arse… get a good actor…
[mumbling to himself as he walks off]…
pretentious little git…

Sebastián can't hide his own self-disgust and deep embarrassment as Anton walks off. Juan catches Sebastián's sensitivity and touches his arm in support.

                    JUAN
Never mind him… drunken old fart!

                    SEBASTIAN
    He's right.

In the distance, Rose [Sebastián's girlfriend] waves at him. There is a big case by her side.

                    SEBASTIAN (CONT'D)
    Rose is leaving for the airport… I've got to go.

BY A TAXI OUTSIDE HOTEL: Sebastián and Rose, highly emotional, hug for a long moment. They look into each other's eyes as she touches his cheek.

                    ROSE
    [Tenderly, English] Promise me… get enough
    sleep…

He nods sheepishly.

                    SEBASTIAN
    [English] I'm terrified…

                    ROSE
    [English] But you never run. Never… [Pause] I
    love that about you, Sebastián.

One last intimate hug before she gets into the taxi. Something childlike and vulnerable about him as he watches her leave.

## 6. INT. PRODUCTION OFFICE – DAY

Daniel's figure fills the monitor from the casting tape. His face is filmed from different angles as the assistant asks him questions. [Daniel's eyes, body language, hands, communicate a powerful, if difficult, presence.]

Mixed with the above, studying the tape with great concentration, are Sebastián, Costa and Maria.

                    ASSISTANT'S VOICE
    And after the mines?

DANIEL

Chapare... then the military.

ASSISTANT'S VOICE

How long?

DANIEL

Three years.

ASSISTANT'S VOICE

Give it up?

Long silence. Sense of tension as Daniel considers the question, or perhaps just remembering. At last he shakes his head.

ASSISTANT'S VOICE (CONT'D)
[Chuckling] Why did you leave? Chucked out?

He volunteers nothing more. Daniel holds the assistant's eye without flinching for a long moment.

SEBASTIAN
[Appreciating] Never know what he's going to do next...

ASSISTANT'S VOICE

What do you do now?

DANIEL
Children to feed... you name it... builder, driver, part-time security...

ASSISTANT'S VOICE

Who for?

DANIEL

President of our Co-operative... where we live...

ASSISTANT'S VOICE

Needs protection... Why?

Daniel smiles unexpectedly. Long pause.

DANIEL

Speaks his mind... that's why.

52

Sebastián freezes on Daniel's face.

> SEBASTIAN
> Look at his eyes… lines on his face…the way he holds himself…

> MARIA
> He draws you in…

> SEBASTIAN
> He's got something… I can smell it…

> COSTA
> Smell trouble! Never acted in his life before… What about the Peruvian actor?

> SEBASTIAN
> Predictable… bland… the easy choice.

> COSTA
> [Staring at Daniel's image] He's a time bomb… can you imagine him on set?! Cocalero, ex-miner, ex-military… rabble rouser! That's all we need…

> SEBASTIAN
> I want him… and his girl…

> COSTA
> Fuck! You sort it out when it blows up in your face! Be warned!

Costa marches out in frustration as Sebastián stares at Daniel's face on screen.

> SEBASTIAN
> [To Maria, but still staring at Daniel's image] He's right… but the film comes first. Always.

## 7. INT. THATCHED PORCH. INDIAN VILLAGE – 15TH CENTURY

The cross of the opening scene, huge and imposing, sits on a hill above the village. In the foreground a group of three or four children whisper to each other. Belen, playing PANUCA, is among them.

They sneak up to the porch, and fascinated, listen to Columbus.

Columbus and some of his men are gathered in a spacious porch. They receive a group of Indian leaders. Daniel, playing Indian rebel HATUEY, is one of them. Anton does this scene with terrific power and presence – real brilliance.

Columbus, who is with a translator [translating simultaneously from Spanish to Quechua] hands out food on a tray to the Indians as he speaks. Hatuey [Daniel] stares at him.

### COLUMBUS
As Governor of this Island I would like to thank you for coming to meet me... After my first voyage I spoke personally with Our Majesties, who have instructed me to treat you with respect and friendship... We request that you recognise the Church and Pope as rulers of the universe... and in turn accept the King and Queen of Spain as rulers of this land... [Murmurs of dissent amongst Indian leaders] If you do so, we shall receive you with love and charity...

He lays down the tray and picks up two little hawk bells and starts fidgeting with them.

### HATUEY
And if we do not?

Columbus moves closer and stares into his face. Both men confront each other for a long moment.

Sebastián and Costa are watching the scene on the combo screen. Columbus and Hatuey are still eye to eye.

> COLUMBUS
> …We shall enslave you and dispose of you as seems fit; we shall seize your possessions and do you as much harm as we can…

> COSTA
> Take my hat off to you… I wouldn't have touched them with a barge poll…

A smile between them. Sebastián's eyes are glued to the screen, appreciating them.

> HATUEY
> What do you want from us?

Columbus raises the little hawk bell and gently tinkles it.

> COLUMBUS
> Taxes! Every Indian over fourteen must fill a bell…

> HATUEY
> With what?

> COLUMBUS
> Gold. [Handing one to Hatuey] It's not very big.

## 8. INT. TENT, LUNCH – DAY

High energy. Cast and crew are in the midst of a lunch break. Colonialists [in costume, some dressed as 'gentlemen' while others look poor or criminal] and Indians, with T-shirts over their minimalist costumes, are all mixed up with the crew.

Anton in the food queue, studies Sebastián seated in a corner with Daniel. They are in deep discussion over something. Sebastián listens to what he says carefully then nods. Daniel says something else and both laugh heartily between themselves till Daniel moves off to another seat elsewhere. Costa now joins Sebastián to discuss a change to the schedule.

Anton, with his tray of food, spots his chance and strides over to an empty seat in front of Sebastián.

He drops an envelope in front of Sebastián which kills the
conversation between Sebastián and Costa immediately.

> ANTON
> I've made a few changes to my scene.

Costa nudges Sebastián with his elbow [to suggest 'cool it'] as
Sebastián's face colours in immediate fury.

> SEBASTIAN
> Who the fuck do you think you are?

> ANTON
> The first man to cross the Atlantic… a mere
> detail I know… but I wish you'd give me a little
> credit…

> SEBASTIAN
> I don't give a flying fuck if he was a good sailor!

The outburst attracts attention from others at the tables close by.

> ANTON
> A little objectivity…

> SEBASTIAN
> Bullshit… doesn't exist! I've got two hours to
> play with… I have to choose just fifty scenes
> from five hundred years ago…

> ANTON
> Ah manipulation?

> SEBASTIAN
> Selection! Which I will defend!… What the fuck
> do you think film is… what do you think history
> is?!

> ANTON
> [Revelling in Sebastián's reaction] Ah… now
> we're getting somewhere!… Would you have the
> guts to confront seventeen shiploads of frenzied
> desperadoes lusting for gold?!… The second
> voyage full of speculators… knights… who
> despised him. What would you have done?

Colonialists from other tables are now listening.

SEBASTIAN

Who cares?!

ANTON

[Pointing at some of his scruffier actors around him] And the dirt poor from Extremadura?... Lived through famine... abused, humiliated by masters... brutalised in wars against the Moors... the Turks... Italy too... Their one and only chance to escape misery... on the backs of the Indians... Well I'd do the fucking same... dog eat dog...

Again Costa whispers to Sebastián that he should calm down. Anton downs another long sip of wine.

ANTON (CONT'D)

'There but for the grace of God...' [Pause] In your blood too...

SEBASTIAN

Fuck off Anton...

ANTON

'Adventure'... [Pointing at him] addicted... another dreamer like Columbus... You're a gambler! You don't do a film like this for money... [Pause, whispered, intense]... You'd sell your own child to get this made... [eye to eye] Wouldn't you?

SEBASTIAN

Played too many parts...

ANTON

Believe me... far too many.

Anton pushes the envelope a little closer which makes Sebastián's temper rise again.

ANTON (CONT'D)
Ruthless little fucker... but you've got balls kid... I'll give you that.

Anton stands up. He leaves his uneaten food behind him but grabs his glass of wine. Close by [but still with a view of Sebastián] he plops himself down opposite Daniel.

ANTON (CONT'D)
Tell me Daniel [with Sebastián still staring at him] What's it like to be a real Indian?

Costa grabs Sebastián's arm as the latter springs up in fury while Daniel takes it as a joke and just laughs.

COSTA
[Whisper] Cool it...

Sebastián flicks the envelope towards Costa.

SEBASTIAN
Throw that in the fucking bin!

Costa snaps up the envelope and tears it open. He pulls out a blank sheet of paper. Sebastián stares at it for a moment in amazement. Costa chuckles.

COSTA
He's just winding you up...

Sebastián's eyes flash at Anton who is now staring across at him with a big mischievous grin on his face. Sebastián's fury gives way to confusion, and then a hint of a chuckle at his own expense. He then to starts to laugh.

SEBASTIAN
The bastard... [staring at Anton now joking with Daniel]... that was a beauty... he really got me.

## 9. EXT. BY THE SETTLEMENT – DAY

Maria takes advantage of a break to continue with the 'Making Of'. In the background the set is being prepared for a new scene. Close-up of a dynamic and passionate Alberto.

>ALBERTO/BARTOLOME
>My character 'Bartolomé de las Casas' lived till he was ninety-two! In those days! Arrived in the Indies at eighteen to take charge of a plantation of Indian slaves… traumatised by what he witnessed… devoted every moment of his life thereafter to the Indian cause… became a Dominican… criss-crossed the Atlantic several times… nearly assassinated on two occasions… an amazing man who on his deathbed… [Genuinely enthused, now quotes from his notebook] Listen to this… 'condemned the blindness of those who ignored genocide and those who give the world orders'. [Pause] Could be today…

His frustration suddenly overcomes him.

>ALBERTO/BARTOLOME (CONT'D)
>Fuck! Fuck! Fuck! Turn that camera off… This guy was the father of International Law, and I've only got eight scenes! Wrote dozens of books… not vanity but this entire film should be about me…

CUT TO:

Close-up of Juan playing Montesinos.

>JUAN/MONTESINOS
>My character's name is Antonio Montesinos… [he freezes, long pause]… Jesus… Sebastián's given me about twenty books to read… in one ear out the other… I'm not a 'book' guy just an actor… this film's supposed to span thirty years and I'm all confused with the bloody dates…

> But I'll tell you this… my character isn't as famous as Bartolomé but he's far more interesting… I spoke up for the Indians first! Gave that famous first sermon in 1511 they tried to ban…[melodramatically] 'I am the voice crying out in the desert… you are in mortal sin!' Assassinated as well by the way… four fucking scenes is all I've got!

CUT TO:

### 10. INT. FILM BASE, COSTUME AREA – DAY ('MAKING OF')

A stunning actress, late thirties, EMMA, already in costume and now getting hair and make-up done. Belen is beside her, besotted, running her hand over her costume. Emma runs an affectionate hand over her cheek and speaks to camera.

> **EMMA**
> [Conspiratorial tone] Just between us… I feel very uncomfortable… I've been imposed by the financiers and the director isn't amused… don't blame him… [as they fix her stunning wig] The actual scene took place between Las Casas and King Ferdinand on his deathbed in 1516… but now it will be with 'moi', Queen Isabella, instead, who died in 1504…

> **MARIA (MAKING OF)**
> That's only twelve years…

> **EMMA**
> Think anyone will notice?

She giggles at the splendid image of herself in a little hand mirror.

> **EMMA (CONT'D)**
> Who cares? [blowing herself a kiss] I look gorgeous [to Belen]. Don't I?

Belen nods in total agreement.

CUT TO: FILM BASE – SET

Torrential rain. It falls heavily on to the thatched roofs of the set, forming puddles and streamlets amongst the lights which are covered by plastic. The crew wait around, chatting, seated on tables in a dining room rigged up in a tent. Sebastián paces up and down, frustrated and tense. His eye catches Costa's; Costa speaks on the phone, seated in a corner, lap-top open in front of him. Anton, by the door, contemplating the rain, looks pensive. In a corner Maria carries on with her 'Making Of'.

We see Belen through Maria's camera, clad in fifteenth century clothing, seated beside Alberto and his huge pile of books. Alberto holds up his book while Belen reads from it.

### BELEN
[Reading, as the others watch] 'Indians feel neither love nor shame... to kill or be killed is all the same to them... they have no knowledge of the all powerful God and worship the devil in all his forms... but Satan has been expelled from the island now that most of the Indians are dead... Who can deny that the use of gunpowder against pagans is like the burning of incense to our Lord?'

Belen looks at them.

### BELEN (CONT'D)
Did someone really write this?

### ALBERTO
The best known historian of his day... famous in Spain.

### MARIA
[To Belen] What do you think?

She hesitates.

### BELEN
But did he know any Indians?

Maria and others are impressed by the question. Costa looks at her. Something about her makes him smile.

## 11. EXT. BY DANIEL'S HOME AND BARRIO, COCHABAMBA – DAY

Belen is in a completely different world. Other children are around her as she stares into the camera and talks in a mixture of Spanish and Quechua.

>MARIA (OFF)
>Why do you want to be an actress, Belen?
>
>BELEN
>I want to be on the TV... learn to sing...
>dance... travel and have a swimming pool...

Dusty, unfinished barrio on the slopes of the hills overlooking the city and mountains beyond. Maria's camera randomly catches the faces of children and labourers.

She now focuses on some DOZEN LABOURERS, spare, wiry bodies, and thick hands from physical work, who are in the process of digging a trench. Two of the labourers drink water from an old rusty barrel. Daniel is among them, with a short metal crowbar in his hand. The men joke with Daniel who laughs easily at their banter. Daniel feels self-conscious as Maria asks him questions.

Only one man, with a tough grizzled face, LABOURER 4, doesn't participate in the general bonhomie. He studies proceedings with deep distrust.

>MARIA (MAKING OF)
>Daniel, why are you doing this film?
>
>DANIEL
>What do you mean?
>
>MARIA
>What most attracted you to the part? Defiance of
>the Indian people? Some sense of settling scores
>after five centuries of lies... what got you?

Daniel just stares at her.

> LABOURER 1
> The cash!

Laughter from all.

> LABOURER 4
> How much are they going to pay you Daniel?

Daniel stiffens a little but ignores the question. An older charismatic man, ENRIQUE, approaches; he joins the mischief and teases Daniel too.

> ENRIQUE
> What if you have to take your clothes off man?

Laughter from the men in the trench; Maria catches their fun.

> LABOURER 1
> [Quechua to Daniel] Like Tarzan... with a little patch over your bollocks!

Guffaws as one of the men beats his chest like Tarzan.

> LABOURER 2
> Any love scenes?

> LABOURER 3
> And the Oscar goes to... Best billy goat shagger in Latin America!

More laughter at Daniel's expense as the men continue to take the piss.

> ENRIQUE
> [To Maria] Hope you don't go putting ideas in his head. I need this man.

Maria directs her camera at him. Enrique takes out a coca leaf and offers it to the men, who take a break from work.

> MARIA
> Do you work together?

                          DANIEL
          [Indicating Enrique] The slave driver! Used to be
          our local headmaster till he got fired... [More
          chuckles from the men] He's now President of
          our Cooperative of five hundred families... we
          built all these houses ourselves...

                         ENRIQUE
          Want to give us a hand? Here's a shovel.

                          MARIA
          Not with these delicate little fingers...

More comments [some in Quechua] and good-natured banter.

                    MARIA (CONT'D)
          What are you digging here?

                         ENRIQUE
          [Pointing below] We're running out of water...
          See that hill... Our community bought a well
          behind there... seven kilometres away...

                          DANIEL
          We're laying a pipe to bring the water over the
          hill and down the slope into our homes...

                    MARIA (MAKING OF)
          Seven kilometres!
                         ENRIQUE
          Now they want to take it from us... privatise
          our water...

An older labourer [number 3] in the trench, covered in dust, body glistening with sweat, looks up at them. He has a quite striking face. The joking stops. They all go deadly serious.

                       LABOURER 3
          Let them try... I'll kill the fuckers.

Labourer 4 smiles for the first time.

> LABOURER 4
> [To camera, in Quechua] What the hell are you doing here?

There is something menacing about his presence as he stares into the camera. Another labourer translates his question.

> MARIA (MAKING OF)
> A documentary about the film…

Labourer 4 looks up from the trench, staring at Daniel.

> LABOURER 4
> [Quechua] Don't trust the fuckers Daniel… I'm warning you…

Suddenly a Jeep pulls up some thirty metres from them. Four men in distinctive company uniforms tentatively get out of the vehicle. One has a clipboard in his hand and looks around him as though searching for something.

Maria is stunned to see Daniel sprint towards them. He shouts at them viciously in Quechua but she can't understand the words; but the driver of their vehicle does. One of the men tries to reason with Daniel. A mistake. Daniel obviously tells them to piss off. More hesitation from the company men.

Daniel, with fearsome energy, suddenly smashes the windscreen of their vehicle and pounds the bodywork with the crowbar. He clobbers the other windows too. The terrified men jump into the vehicle which continues to take a pounding. The vehicle spins off as more windows are smashed in.

Daniel, with a darkness in his eye, glances at his shocked friends and then disappears into the warren of little alleyways among the humble homes.

The Jeep drives past Maria and she notices the logo on the side: 'Spring Water Incorporated'.

## 12. INT. EXPENSIVE RESTAURANT, COCHABAMBA – NIGHT

Old-fashioned but expensive restaurant. Once again the waiters are dressed in pristine uniforms and hover, almost invisibly, around the table. The meal is over, but plates are littered with leftover food in substantial quantities.

Sebastián, Costa, Anton, Alberto, Juan, Maria and Emma and several other actors are all present. All have enjoyed a good drink – they are still at it – and it shows in the way they speak.

[Emma and Juan sitting opposite each other, keep eyeing each other throughout the scene.]

They are now sipping brandies, and some of them smoke cigars. Anton has had far too much to drink; he is in a dark mood and determined to provoke. Conversation is in passionate full flow. Overlapping voices and sense of real debate going on.

Occasionally a young waiter by the table is summoned by a quick gesture and a glass is pointed at for filling as the conversation continues. He has sharp eyes and he listens carefully to the discussion as he pours.

Alberto, seated between Emma and the assistant, jokes with the same waiter and asks him what the Quechua word is for various pieces of cutlery and food on the table. [Glass, fork, spoon, meat, water, with word for water – Yaku – repeated various times.] Alberto, with Emma and the assistant chipping in too, copies the words as best they can as some of the young waiters and others are entertained by the innocent and good-natured exchange.

But Anton's mood darkens.

> ANTON/COLUMBUS
> [As if charming]… Nothing like getting into character… God Bless you Father… [To Alberto, friendly but fiercely cruel] Ask for a plastic box… fill it all up with this wasted food that cost more than his month's salary… and bring it out

to his emaciated little children who will gobble it
all up like hungry rodents! Then you'll really feel
like a missionary!

                        EMMA
            [Incredulous] Bitter old wanker...

                        ASSISTANT
            Anton... relax!... It's Saturday night!

                        ANTON
            [Stinging] Tell me... how long do you think
            you'll remember the word 'Yaku'?

Alberto gives him the finger.

                        ANTON (CONT'D)
            Ohhh... not very saint-like... but director here
            will cut that out too... just like [to Sebastián,
            making sure he hears] Las Casas called for black
            slaves from the African coast to replace
            Indians!... Why not have that in the fucking
            story?!

Sense of injustice and scoffing from the others. Costa is amazed at his capacity to provoke and his eyes scan the rising temperature, between checking texts on his Blackberry.

                        COSTA
            [To Sebastián] Christ... he's doing it again...

It calms Sebastián slightly.

                        SEBASTIAN
            In his youth, for a very short time.

But it infuriates Alberto.

                        ALBERTO/BARTOLOME
            [Above Anton's scorn] Las Casas regretted it for
            the rest of my life!

Maria and Sebastián catch a look at each other in response to the passionate defence.

ANTON
What about your deal with slave traders?

ALBERTO
A disaster that shamed him!

ANTON
Getting your holy knickers in a twist Reverend...

ALBERTO
Till his last breath he exposed corrupt Bishops, merchants, royal officials... they hated him!

Maria and Sebastián continue to enjoy it.

ALBERTO (CONT'D)
He declared Indians had been sacrificed, quote, 'to private appetites and private profit'! Five hundred years ago! On his deathbed at ninety-two he lit a candle and swore before Christ that what he had written was all true... And cynics like you want to reduce his entire life to one mistake!

ANTON
Like football... history is cruel to losers.

Some are outraged, but others laugh and appreciate the dark humour.

JUAN/MONTESINOS
Cut that poisoned old fucker out... [laughter]... make the film about me!

ANTON/COLUMBUS
[Holding Bartolomé's eye] You never questioned Spanish authority over the New World... nor the authority of the King... in other words... you were a conservative!

The young waiter listens carefully as Columbus holds Bartolomé's eye. Real heat between them.

**ALBERTO/BARTOLOME**
A radical! He demanded 'equal' treatment with the Spanish for Christ's sake...

**ANTON/COLUMBUS**
Under the Crown!

**ALBERTO/BARTOLOME**
Only with Indian consent! Still hundreds of years ahead of my time!

**COSTA**
How the fuck did Disney pass on this?

Laughter. It dies down. A few drinks are taken.

**EMMA/QUEEN ISABELLA**
[Sweetly] And what about the Protestant Reformation?

It stuns them all into silence. They all turn to look at her.

**COSTA**
Thank you Your Majesty.... that's the sequel.

More uproar. [handwritten: Mehr Aufregung]

**EMMA/QUEEN ISABELLA**
[Above the laughter] I'm serious!... We can't understand Spain without the Reformation!

**ANTON/COLUMBUS**
[To Sebastián] You have an agenda... [indicating Bartolomé and Montesinos] Sanctify these two fuckers and string me up! This isn't art... it's agitprop!

**ALBERTO/BARTOLOME**
So why the hell are you doing it?

**ANTON/COLUMBUS**
For gold! [They laugh] And Christ.

Sebastián appreciates his wit despite the bitterness underneath.

>                    JUAN/MONTESINOS
> [Straight face] Can I just say something...
> [melodramatic] 'I am the voice of one in the
> desert of this island...
>
>                    ALL TOGETHER
> 'You are in mortal sin!'

Even Anton chuckles. Emma and Juan stare at each other across the table.

### 13. INT. SEBASTIAN'S ROOM – NIGHT

Sebastián, late at night, is surrounded by notes, books and pieces of paper. He sketches forthcoming scenes beautifully with great skill. He becomes aware of a rhythmic banging sound on the wall beside him. He stops and listens carefully, then a smile comes to his face as he shakes his head.

### 14. INT. ROOM NEXT DOOR – NIGHT

Emma, the Catholic Queen, bonks for Spain as she flattens the poor prelate beneath her.

>                    JUAN/MONTESINOS
> [Groaning, coming] Ahh Ahh Ahh...fuck... sorry
> Your Highness...
>
>                    EMMA/QUEEN
> Another useless priest... I should have shagged
> Hatuey.

They laugh and lie back in bed.

### 15. EXT. CORPORATE HQ OF WATER COMPANY – AFTERNOON

An imposing building with perhaps a little plaza before it. A proud company logo [the same that was on 4 x 4 attacked by Daniel] dominates the entrance to the building.

Just in front of the building is a big flagpole, with a striking company flag [same logo] fluttering above in the breeze. A row of private security guards are lined up in front of the building, and look down on a lively crowd gathered around the flagpole. There is both laughter and spontaneous applause from them as they listen to a lively public speaker with a microphone.

CLOSER: The crowd is entertained by Enrique, Co-op President [with Daniel as bodyguard], who is at the centre of a group of water activists who hand out leaflets and engage with those interested.

Costa watches carefully as Maria records them.

>COSTA
>What the fuck is Daniel doing there?

>MARIA
>His bodyguard, remember?... [Camera now focuses in close on Enrique] Listen to this guy... he's amazing...

[Enrique has a fine turn of phrase and it's obvious he is used to public speaking.] Costa listens and watches several heavily armed policemen with growing concern as they move a little closer.

>ENRIQUE
>[With energy, and comic timing] By what right do the corrupt little 'midgets' in the Town Hall sell to these slimy crooks [indicating HQ behind him]... Against our will they sell off our rivers, our lakes, our wells... not only that... the aquifers below us... and the rain above us!... By law!... Beyond belief... [Pause, power] we cannot collect the rain! And who claims our rain?...[Pointing above at the flag] A company in the tax-dodging Cayman Islands... whose real masters are in London and California! What are they going to steal next?... The vapour from our breath? The sweat from our brow?... All they'll get from me [pregnant pause, great timing, with pelvic thrust] is piss!

Lots of laughter and applause. The police move closer.

> ENRIQUE (CONT'D)
> Welcome Officers!... [Daniel moves closer to
> Enrique]... Rest your weary truncheons!

They are embarrassed by his wit and the laughter of the crowd.

> ENRIQUE (CONT'D)
> I hope you'll join us to burn the water bills in
> the Town Square... because that's what we are
> going to do when we get them!
> [Applause]
> Mark my words... [indicating] this flag... we are
> going to tear it down!

Another cheer. On impulse a young lad begins to climb the pole. As he climbs higher a security guard grabs him by the leg and pulls him down. Daniel aggressively rushes forward and in a flash has the security man's arm up his back. Others guards are about to intervene until Enrique calms it all down by indicating that Daniel should let the man go.

> ENRIQUE (CONT'D)
> Don't worry boys... there'll be a next time!

Laughter again. Camera catches Daniel face to face with another really tough guard. Costa watches Daniel. His anxiety mounts.

> MARIA
> Something really big's going on... they're
> mobilising thousands... People are furious! And
> no wonder... Going to lose their own wells...
> [Trying to tempt him, pause] It could be an
> amazing documentary Costa... let me do it...

> COSTA
> Fuck that!... I won't spend another penny...

> MARIA
> Costa... chance of a lifetime...

                    COSTA
: [Cutting her off] I'm not a fucking NGO! Stay
out of it!

                    MARIA
: This will blow up in your face… I'm warning
you.

Costa stares at Daniel who is now in a heated argument with a security guard from the company.

## 16. EXT. STRAW CHURCH, SETTLEMENT – DAY

A dozen Bolivian workers, some of them Indians, build a simple wooden church, with a thatched roof. Some of them are on scaffolding. Carpenters hammer away. In the midst of all this chaotic activity, Sebastián tries to rehearse with Alberto and Juan, who are playing Bartolomé and Montesinos.

Montesinos, with a Bible in his hand, hovers around a small lectern from which he will give his sermon to the imagined audience. Sebastián's assistant also has a script in his hand.

                    ASSISTANT
: [To the workers] Boys… can you knock it off for
ten minutes… We need a little silence, please…
Thanks very much.

The workers put down their tools but remain at their work positions. Some of them seated on the scaffolding, their legs dangling, look down with some curiosity as the scene unfolds before them. Sebastián sets the scene.

                    SEBASTIAN
: Here we go… March 1511… a lot of tension…
The rich and powerful of the island have been
called to hear a sermon by the Dominican
priests… It was written between them but
Montesinos, the best speaker, was chosen to
preach… [Pointing at Alberto] Bartolomé is
there… but just as another Spaniard with a farm
and Indians…

Alberto/Bartolomé nods as he takes a seat in a wooden bench opposite the altar. Montesinos opens the Bible. Sebastián is standing to one side, following the rehearsal.

> SEBASTIAN (CONT'D)
> Montesinos waits till the hymn finishes, makes brief eye contact with Bartolomé and then begins...

Montesinos gazes out at his imaginary congregation and the real workers on the set.

> MONTESINOS
> 'The Pharisees sent someone to ask St. John the Baptist who he was, and he replied, "'I am the voice crying out in the desert."'

Montesinos snaps the book shut and looks out at the Indian workers.

> MONTESINOS (CONT'D)
> ...Indians mine our gold which builds our cities, even churches... finances further conquests in far distant parts and so the great wheel of 'Commerce' turns... Not one of us is untouched by Indian sweat, least of all His Majesty and his bishops...

Some of the workers glance at each other.

> SEBASTIAN
> [Reading the script] The congregation are stunned. They have never heard anything like this. Growing tension in the air... Montesinos continues.

> MONTESINOS
> As a preacher, I am confronted by Gospel imperatives... the first of which is to preach the truth...

Montesinos glances at the Gospel again.

MONTESINOS (CONT'D)
I am the voice of Christ in the desert of this
island... YOU ARE IN MORTAL SIN!

SEBASTIAN
Terrific! A furious muttering around the church.
The rich are scandalised... Now, you come
down... walk among them... you have real
authority... the angry voice of Christ!

Montesinos makes his way down the small platform and starts walking towards the congregation.

MONTESINOS
Mortal sin! [with great vigour]... you live in it,
you die in it... why? Because of the cruel
tyranny you impose on these innocent people.
Tell me... by what justice do you hold these
Indians in such vile servitude?

Sebastián is totally absorbed by every word.

MONTESINOS (CONT'D)
By what authority have you inflicted such
hideous wars on these people? They were living
in their own lands in peace...

SEBASTIAN
Protests! This is outrageous!

MONTESINOS
By what right do you keep them so oppressed,
starved and exhausted? And they die on you... or
should I say, you murder them!

Sebastián is elated.

SEBASTIAN
More shouting! Some stamp out. It gives you
strength... go for their conscience!

MONTESINOS
How can you be so asleep... so deep inside a
torpid dream...

Some of the workers above are intrigued. Sebastián's eyes shine; he mouths the words in silence completely in sync with Montesinos.

> MONTESINOS (CONT'D)
> Look into an Indian's eyes. Are these not men? Do they not have rational souls? Are you not obliged to love them as yourselves?

> SEBASTIAN
> [Voice from congregation] Who the hell do you think you are?! You're not a priest... you're nothing but a dirty tramp! [To actor Juan] You don't budge... fearless... you confront the screaming faces... the Governor of the island rises to his feet...

> SEBASTIAN/GOVERNOR
> Your sermon today undermined my authority and that of the King... I demand an official retraction Padre Montesinos! Your inflammatory notions will be wiped from memory... today... 11th of March 1511 will no longer exist!

> JUAN/MONTESINOS
> Do I stay at the lectern?

> SEBASTIAN
> Don't move an inch... stare them out... [more lines of dialogue] This is a capital offence! Traitor! Burn the bastard! Back to Spain Montesinos before we cut your tongue out! [To Juan] And then your line above the insults...

> MONTESINOS
> The truth has many enemies... lies have many friends.

He leans forward and kisses the Bible.

> SEBASTIAN
> More shouting... you look at Bartolomé for the

last time... he's overwhelmed... calm and
collected, your head held high... you move back
to the altar... [Juan does that]... that's it...
Fucking great...

### JUAN

[Going over the scene] I really go for it... fuck...
these are the most powerful men on the island...
vicious men...

### SEBASTIAN

[With genuine respect] He never retracted... the
following Saturday he preached again...
denounced them even more... he must have
been an incredible character... quite special...

### JUAN

Who killed him?

### SEBASTIAN

It's a mystery... but some academics think he was
killed by an agent working for a German bank...

### ALBERTO

Jesus! Is that true?

### SEBASTIAN

[Nodding] The first voice of conscience against
an empire... from a little straw church like this...
And here we are... his words come to life again.

Sebastián glances around him. Imagining. A young Indian worker looks down at him from the scaffolding.

### ASSISTANT

[To Alberto and Juan] Costumes boys... [To
Indian workers] Thanks lads... back to work. [To
Sebastián] There's a message for you at the
office... call your girl.

Sebastián nods as the others leave. He takes a seat on a wooden box in the corner and studies the church that's being built before him. His mind flies back five hundred years and he's strangely moved, emotional, as he lives the moments long gone. There is a deep calm and intensity about him. He bows his head, as if saying a quiet prayer to himself; or probably just a small token of respect for the little known Dominican martyr Montesinos.

### 17. INT. PRODUCTION OFFICE – DAY

Sebastián talks to his girlfriend Rose via skype. They speak in English. He hugs the corner as he seeks privacy in a public space. Rose's face fills the computer screen and she is deeply upset.

>ROSE
>I feel so stupid…

She starts to cry.

>SEBASTIAN
>Don't cry Rose…

>ROSE
>It's the wrong time… isn't it?

Long silence. Rose moves and disappears from the screen. We now hear just her voice.

>ROSE (CONT'D)
>I can't even say the word…

Rose walks around, reappears; now just a partial image of her in a corner of the screen.

>SEBASTIAN
>Jesus.… wish I could just hold you.

>ROSE
>I had a dream Sebastián… a little girl sat on the edge of my bed…

>SEBASTIAN
>You'll upset yourself… Don't think like that.

                    ROSE

I kept asking her… 'Who are you? Why have you
come now?' She just looked at me, Sebastián,
with the saddest face… [pause]… and then she
disappeared…

Rose begins to sob and disappears again from the screen. Sebastián stares at the blank space.

                    SEBASTIAN

Rose!

                    ROSE

Sorry… It's all too much for me…

There is a brief glimpse of her before she cuts communication. A dead screen. Sebastián, overwhelmed, shuts his eyes and leans his head back against the wall.

                    SEBASTIAN

Fuck…

### 18. INT. BAR HOTEL, COCHABAMBA – NIGHT

Sebastián is at the bar, nursing a drink by himself. Costa joins him.

                    SEBASTIAN

Everything okay?

Costa nods. Sebastián looks exhausted, and in low spirits.

                    COSTA

What is it?

Sebastián hesitates then it all bursts out in deep frustration.

                    SEBASTIAN

A baby!… Jesus… it's just not the right time!
Look at all the projects we have ahead of us…
we'll be working like dogs… travelling, setting
things up… it sucks up every bit of energy you
have… I need the freedom to work on spec…
take a risk… Costa… I don't want to be an

invisible fucking dad racked with guilt who sees his kid once in a blue moon... I don't want to be a stranger to my own child...

He stops himself as he notices Costa's face.

SEBASTIAN (CONT'D)
Fuck! I'm sorry...

COSTA
It's okay...

They both stare at their drinks for a few moments.

SEBASTIAN
I didn't mean to...

COSTA
It's okay I said...

Another long pause.

SEBASTIAN
I'm a self-centred arsehole... [pause] I don't know why you put up with me...

COSTA
Neither do I...

Sebastián puts his hand over Costa's shoulder. Costa does the same to Sebastián. They knock back their drinks.

COSTA (CONT'D)
[To waiter] Same again... a double.

19. INT. COSTA'S ROOM – NIGHT

Costa lies back on his bed, hands behind his head, eyes wide open, deep in thought. Several long moments of silence. At last there is a knock on the door.

COSTA
It's open.

A beautiful young GIRL enters. She has Indian features and long dark hair. But she seems very young and clearly still an adolescent. Costa stares at her.

> GIRL
> [Poor Spanish] Got your call... It's twenty dollars US. My name's Wendy.

> COSTA
> How old are you?

### 20. INT. WAREHOUSE, FILM BASE – AFTERNOON

Various film crew are hard at work in preparation for forthcoming scenes. Sense of great activity. One corner of the warehouse is full of building materials and props. At another corner, costume.

Daniel and Belen study the wonders of the warehouse. They are fascinated by the various props. Costa approaches. Daniel picks up a hatchet and runs his finger over its sharp edge. Next to him there is a chopping block and other Spanish weapons, an endless array of swords, lances, daggers, shields, muskets, pistols, and cannons; body armour, iron chains for slaves, and helmets.

Daniel picks up a metal instrument he doesn't recognise. [Costa mimics a branding iron on a body and the noise of contact with flesh – 'Shish'.]

> COSTA
> ...I saw you with Enrique and the police the other day... if something happens to you we are fucked... do you realise that?

Daniel just watches him.

> COSTA (CONT'D)
> ...[Glancing round the warehouse] All this work gone to waste... only four weeks left Daniel... please... that's all I ask.

His mobile phone rings. He listens for a few moments as Daniel fingers more props.

                    COSTA (CONT'D)
          [To Daniel, pointing at the phone] Financiers
          calling!... Just seen the rushes... fantastic... you
          look great!

Daniel smiles as Costa slips into English.

                    COSTA (CONT'D)
          [English] I'm with Hatuey here... I was totally
          against him but Sebastián was right...

                    VOICE
          ...Real sense of scale, man... looks like a twenty
          million dollar movie!

Daniel fidgets with the props.

                    COSTA
          [Occasionally looking at Daniel] Amazing, man...
          cheaper to get a man to sit on the lights stand
          than buy a sandbag! Two fucking dollars a day
          and they feel like kings... throw in a few water
          pumps... leave a few clapped-out old trucks
          when you're done... and hey presto... two
          hundred fucking extras!

                    VOICE
          El Cid man!

                    COSTA
          Ben Hur! Keep me posted!

Costa finishes the conversation and turns back to Daniel. He puts his arm round his shoulder as he examines a hawk bell.

                    DANIEL
          They really had to fill this with gold dust?

Costa nods as he takes it in his hand.

                    COSTA
          Colossal scenes coming up... hundreds and
          hundreds of bodies stretching down a ravine
          panning for gold... fucking epic!

                          DANIEL
     Ben Hur…

Costa laughs.

                          COSTA
     You catch on fast!

Daniel moves up to him and looks him straight in the eye.

                          DANIEL
     [In heavily accented English] Two fucking dollars
     a day… [pause]… and we feel like kings…

Costa's jaw drops.

                     DANIEL (CONT'D)
     [Still in English] I worked in a building site in
     New York for three years… till I got caught.
     [Pause] They treated us like dumb animals too.

Costa hangs his head. Belen comes up to them, with something in her hand. She shows it to her father.

                     DANIEL (CONT'D)
     [In Quechua] Put that back…

Daniel about-turns and walks off as Costa melts with shame.

                          BELEN
     What's wrong?

Belen and Costa's eyes meet for a moment before she runs off to join her father.


## 21. HOTEL ROOM – NIGHT

Anton, in baggy shorts and sweaty vest, finishes dialling a number. His door is open and Costa tentatively approaches carrying a script. Anton waves him in.

                          COSTA
     [Holding up the script] Hear you want a hand
     with this?

ANTON
Everybody else too scared?

Anton still has the phone at his ear which continues to ring out. He tries another number and the answering machine clicks on. He hesitates.

ANTON (CONT'D)
It's me... [pause] again. Tried all the numbers [pause] again... would be good to hear from any of you... Have the kids got my number? [Pause, with a glance at Costa] I'm sober in the mornings... usually... Take care. [Pause] I've got something to tell you...

He puts down the phone.

ANTON (CONT'D)
Got family?

Costa hesitates.

COSTA
Fourteen-year-old son. Lives with his mum.

ANTON
How is he?

Costa doesn't answer.

ANTON (CONT'D)
[Almost to himself] This business... fucks up families.

Anton leans over for his script and winces with pain.

COSTA
Something wrong?

Anton ignores him and studies his script. To Costa's surprise the margins are full of detailed notes, scribbles and many questions.

COSTA (CONT'D)
You take it serious...

He can read a fury in Anton's eye at the comment. It subsides.

> ANTON
> It's all I've got…

Suddenly Anton starts pounding his forehead with the palm of his hand. The self-inflicted violence of it all shocks Costa.

> ANTON (CONT'D)
> Can't remember… my fucking brain…

> COSTA
> Anton…

> ANTON
> [Snapping his fingers impatiently] Give me my line!

> COSTA
> [Looking down at the script] They are so artless and so free with all they possess…

Anton, although struggling to remember, continues with great subtlety as he wanders round the room.

> ANTON/COLUMBUS
> …of anything they have, if you ask them for it, they never say no; rather they invite the person to share it, and show as much love as if they were giving their hearts… I have not been able to find out if they have private property. As far as I could see whatever a man had was shared among all the rest. [Pause] With just fifty men they could all be subjected and made to do all that one might wish…

Long pause as Anton fights to remember as he indicates Costa shouldn't give him the line. His frustration grows and at last he gives in. Costa tentatively gives him it.

> COSTA
> …In the first island I found I took some by force…

COLUMBUS
...They have been very 'serviceable'... later I picked up seven head of women and three children. Their Highnesses can see that I shall give them as much gold as they want if they will render me a little help... besides spice and cotton, there are slaves, as many as they shall order...

Again he fights with himself. He downs a long glug of whisky.

COSTA
[Prompting]... All Christendom ought to feel joyful...

COLUMBUS
...and give solemn thanks to the Holy Trinity in turning so many peoples to our holy faith... [somehow with a understated fury] and afterwards for material benefits, since not only Spain but all Christians will hence have refreshment and [pause, savouring it] profit...

Long silence.

COSTA
Nobody speaks like this... no wonder you can't remember...

ANTON
It was his very 'first' letter back from the New World to the Spanish Crown... who in turn forwarded it to their friend Rodrigo de Borja... a big fat glutton... [pause] and Pope... who signed a Papal bull signing over the entire New World to the Spanish Crown...

COSTA
[Snapping his fingers] Just like that.

ANTON
Why Sebastián is so keen on the exact text… I don't know if it will work… He takes risks… I admire the boy for trying…

Anton takes another drink.

COSTA
[Looking down on the script] 'Seven head of women'… [Long pause] I wonder what their names were?

Anton stares at him.

ANTON
What are you doing here?

COSTA
Known Sebastián for a long time… gave me my first break… our third film together… this is a big jump for us…

ANTON
[Slapping his script] But what about this?

Costa stares back at him.

COSTA
I don't give a fuck what happened yesterday never mind five hundred years ago.

A moment between them. Anton smiles as he recognises his honesty.

COSTA (CONT'D)
Why are you drinking so much Anton?

ANTON
I am very very very [pause] thirsty.

COSTA
Are you going to get through this? We're fucked without you…

A moment between them.

ANTON
Nice to feel needed… [pause]… suggest you
start saying your prayers.

## 22. EXT. INDIAN VILLAGE/PROJECTION ROOM, HOTEL – DAY

[A period scene, with sharp cuts, and glimpses of the clapperboard between takes, mixed with a projection room.]

The team [Sebastián, director of photography, assistant, Maria, and several others too] view the rushes. The shots have been set in order and edited in such a way that, though 'unfinished', the scene still has dramatic shape to the viewer.

Costa sits beside Belen who is held spellbound by the magic of film. Anton is there too, watching in silence. The scene alternates between the period action on screen, and the faces of those watching. Belen, so caught up by the images, grips Costa's arm without noticing. An ease between them.

ON SCREEN – RUSHES:

A queue of some fifty exhausted Indians by one of the bigger thatched buildings, under the watchful eye of several soldiers. At the head of that queue there is an improvised writing table around which five or six officials are congregated along with helpers armed with scales, weights, paper and other odds and ends. The Indians come forward in two separate queues. On the other side of the building, the sounds of yelping dogs.

Great fear and tension on Indian faces as more Indians are rounded up and shoved into the queue by soldiers. Now the face of Belen/Panuca, who is towards the head of the queue with her [actor] father.

ROOM: Belen is stunned to see her own image on the screen for the first time, and Costa can't help but be touched by her youthful wonder.

ON SCREEN: Panuca and her father pay close attention to what's going on ahead of them. An Indian in queue 1 offers his hawk's bell. A SPANIARD carefully takes it and empties the contents into a bowl. A simple metal token is stamped and subsequently hung around his neck.

An INDIAN in queue 2 hands over his bell. The Spaniard upturns the bell into a small dish; there is hardly any gold and it is heavily adulterated with sand. The soldier speaks to the Indians in Spanish without bothering to find out if they understand the language.

>  SPANIARD (OFF)
> Do you think I'm stupid!

He whacks the Indian powerfully across the face, and then tries to separate sand from gold.

>  SPANIARD (CONT'D)
> Have him clipped.

Two smiling soldiers grab him.

The Indian looks at them, terrified, while the two soldiers push him, out of frame. Snap of the clapperboard.

In a new shot, Panuca's father, with his girl at his side; with growing panic Panuca notices the small amount of gold in her father's bell. A Spaniard upturns the bell and is furious at the tiny amount left lying on a dish.

>  SPANIARD (CONT'D)
> [To other soldiers] Take him!

ROOM: Again, Belen's face: she is moved, totally absorbed in the screen.

In another shot, Panuca follows her father round to the back of the building.

POV PANUCA. BEHIND THE BUILDING:

There are two groups of Spanish soldiers working together. They are casual but businesslike as they hover round a bloodstained chopping block. One is sharpening an axe, checking the blade with his thumb. One of the soldiers grabs Panuca's father's arm and holds it out along the bloody block. His arm is placed along it.

Back to Panuca, who screams and runs towards her father.

> PANUCA
> [In Quechua] No! Father!

She is intercepted by a soldier who grabs her arm. Panuca screams and fights but the soldier, laughing, is too strong.

Shot of Columbus and his Captain who appear round the corner.

> PANUCA (CONT'D)
> [Shouting at Columbus, in Quechua] Tell him to stop!

Columbus doesn't intervene. Panuca shrieks as the soldier raises the axe above his shoulder. Her father bows his head. Still on Columbus's face… We only hear the thud of axe on wood and horrendous screams from father and daughter.

Back to Panuca, crying disconsolately, calling out to her father in her own language. The soldier releases her and she collapses to the ground.

ROOM: The screening finishes.

Belen is visibly shaken. Costa hugs her affectionately and winks at her.

> COSTA
> You were brilliant.

Sebastián leans over to her and gives her the thumbs up.

Whispers of approval and quiet comments in the room.

Anton, deep in thought, still stares at the blank screen Sebastián pats Anton on the shoulder too in appreciation. Sebastián heads off with other members of the crew. Anton approaches Costa who is making his way out with Belen.

> ANTON
> [To Costa] And all those statues to the 'Great Man'… Funny how a little mutilation is so quickly forgotten.

Costa and Anton hold each other's eye for a moment.

> ANTON (CONT'D)
> [To Belen, genuinely tender] You have talent… you should be proud… Hope they are paying you properly…

> BELEN
> A fortune! More than the extras…

> ANTON
> Know how much they are paying me? I'll tell you… come here…

Costa watches them leave.

OUTSIDE THE ROOM: Daniel is waiting for Belen, who goes up to him. Costa and Daniel's eyes meet. Daniel, no time for politeness, looks away. Costa watches father and daughter head off in animated conversation in Quechua.

### 23. EXT/INT. DANIEL'S HOUSE – NIGHT

Costa calls at the door to Daniel's house. Belen opens the door. She is surprised. She calls her father, who comes out.

> COSTA
> I owe you an apology.

Daniel holds his eyes for a long moment.

MEAL – LATER:

Costa eats with Daniel and family around a simple table in the humblest of surroundings. Belen is there with her two older brothers.

TERESA, Daniel's wife, makes sure she serves Costa water from a bought plastic bottle while the others are served from a barrel by jug.

Relaxed atmosphere. Costa enjoys the meal and jokes with Teresa as she tries to give him extra. A moment between Daniel and Costa across the table.

COSTA (CONT'D)
That was a feast... thank you.

### 24. INT. 4 X 4, BOLIVIAN COUNTRYSIDE – DAY

Sebastián's 4 x 4, in convoy with other vehicles, speeds through spectacular countryside.

Inside the 4 x 4: Sebastián in the front seat, but mentally elsewhere. With a deep feeling of disquiet, his eyes are glued to the script on his knee. He turns the pages quickly, and his imagination is flying...

### 25. EXT. COUNTRYSIDE – DAY (15TH CENTURY)

Four Spaniards rest under an enormous tree. [Their horses are tied up behind them.] They joke among themselves as they pass around a leather water pouch. The second Spaniard lifts the pouch above his head and the clear liquid, every drop, is now greedily consumed; silence, apart from his Adam's apple bobbing with every deep, satisfied, noisy gulp.

The terrible thud of an arrow suddenly sinking into his throat, giving rise to another terrible gurgle... He dies within seconds.

The other three are also struck down by spears and arrows. One arrow bounces off the armour of the fourth Spaniard and he makes to run. He is intercepted by Hatuey [Daniel] who lays into him with a wooden club. He collapses in a heap.

Hatuey, accompanied by another Indian, now moves to the next tree. Some fifty Indians are roped together at the neck, women and babies among them.

The smallest children are tied in bunches of five. Among them, Panuca... Some of the men have been carrying enormous piles of produce.

They look at him in total awe.

Hatuey, club in hand, moves towards them.

                    HATUEY
        I'll die on my feet. Not on my knees!

Hatuey and the others with him begin to cut the ropes holding the captured Indians.

                    HATUEY (CONT'D)
        [To all the Indians] This island is dead. We are
        going across to Cuba… and will fight on from
        there.

The Indians hesitate. Some of them join him.

                    WOMAN
        What are we going to do with our children?

Hatuey has no answer.

                    WOMAN (CONT'D)
        I won't have them thrown to the dogs!

He can't bear the anguish on her face.

                    HATUEY
        We must go. Now!

CUT TO:

Flash of bodies. Indians, young and old, running through the countryside… Distant sound of yelping dogs getting closer and closer.

Hatuey helps them across a river, whispering words of encouragement to terrified faces. An old woman scrambles across with some help, but she is struggling.

PATHS: terrified Indians run as fast as they can. Deep breaths, panting chests… They reach a fork. Hatuey orders some to go right and others left.

More fear and terror on their faces as they split from friends and loved ones and run on… The horrific yelps growing stronger…

BEHIND: Half a dozen Spanish mastiffs [the two favourites with leather armour around their bodies] and armed Spanish settlers charge in hot pursuit.

Sensing blood, the dogs surge forward in frenzied anticipation, sniffing rabidly around the fork in the road.

BY THE INDIANS: Horrific yelping in the distance; horrified bodies dashing along the paths. The older ones, their lungs bursting with the effort, are dragged by their younger counterparts.

Hatuey urges them on.

CLEARING IN THE FOREST: An OLDER WOMAN collapses, out of sheer exhaustion. She gestures to the others to run on. A YOUNGER WOMAN, with a child in her arms, pulls desperately at her.

> YOUNG WOMAN
> [Indian language] Mother… get up! Mother! I'll help you! Up! We can't stop now…

The sound of the howling dogs getting closer and closer.

Hatuey hesitates. He grabs the baby out of the younger woman's arms, taking it into his own, then grabs the young woman and tries to drag her along. But she doesn't budge.

He speaks to her quietly but desperately. Still she won't move. Yelps getting closer and closer…

He decides to drag her along violently as they leave the old woman behind.

> YOUNG WOMAN (CONT'D)
> Mother!

They have one last glimpse of her as they disappear along the path.

The dogs bound closer.

The old woman sits by herself.

OLD WOMAN'S POV, ground-level in the clearing: Terrifying. She pulls herself up into a sitting position. She wipes a bit of dirt from her leg. She takes a deep breath and tries to calm herself.

The last few moments of her life… Her old eyes and frail body… Her entire life flashes before her.

She looks up.

From her POV the first of a pack of dogs, teeth bared, leaps towards her.

BY HATUEY, on a path: In the distance they hear a crescendo of howls and screaming. The young woman wails and collapses. Hatuey drops to his knees and holds her tight as she sobs her heart out…

CUT TO: 4 x 4:

A perturbed look on Sebastián's face, a hint of reddening eyes as he looks up from his script, shuts it, lays his hand on it, and leans his head on the window of the 4 x 4 as the countryside flashes past in a blur.

### 26. EXT. SET, BY THE RIVER, POOL – DAY

In hushed tones, Sebastián, helped by Daniel, speaks to five young mothers [some of the faces recognisable from above] who clutch their babies in their arms. They are a few steps from the water. Sebastián speaks with great sensitivity and respect. The women listen carefully, but there is a sense of growing disquiet among them, which only increases as the scene progresses.

> SEBASTIAN
> …It was a heart-breaking choice… horrific…
> they couldn't face the thought of being caught
> by the dogs…

The women look at each other and grip their babies tighter. One of them glances across at a dog handler with a mastiff and looks visibly moved.

> SEBASTIAN (CONT'D)
> …So we'll see you talk to Hatuey… you realise
> there's no escape… and then you have to take
> the terrible decision… You do it together to find

> strength in each other... You'll wade into the
> water with your babies... you'll all be crying and
> wailing... and then you'll throw your babies into
> the water and drown them...

The women are upset and their faces darken. One turns to the water. Two others start speaking to each other very quietly in their own language.

> SEBASTIAN (CONT'D)
> ...First take we'll just see you go into the water
> with your own babies... after that, we'll swap the
> babies for the dolls... What's wrong, Daniel?

Daniel and the women start speaking to each other in quiet, worried tones. A debate takes place between them.

> SEBASTIAN (CONT'D)
> [With deep concern] We've got to show what
> really happened... I'm not making it up...

> DANIEL
> That's not the problem...

Daniel, with great patience, goes back to the women. The women seem very upset even at the thought of it and the argument heightens.

> DANIEL (CONT'D)
> Sebastián... give them some time to think about
> it...

> SEBASTIAN
> We explained this all before... their babies won't
> even get wet... they go up to their waists and we
> stop... Look... we have the dolls all ready...

> DANIEL
> Sebastián... please...

Sebastián, trying to control his mounting frustration, decides to give them some breathing space and heads off to a rock and sits down.

Costa and the entire crew have witnessed the mounting crisis. [Props have the dolls ready and costume are ready with towels.] Costa joins Sebastián.

Belen then joins Costa, sitting beside him. Together they watch the quiet discussion between the women and Daniel.

One mother is particularly upset and begins to cry.

The crew are stunned as they watch the drama from a distance.

Eventually Daniel comes over to Sebastián.

> DANIEL (CONT'D)
> I'm sorry Sebastián... they won't do it... they can't bear the thought...

> SEBASTIAN
> You know why this is so important... I've got to get it done!

Daniel stares at him for a moment.

> DANIEL
> There are more important things than your film.

Daniel goes back to the women and they leave the set together. Sebastián buries his head in his hands, bursting with frustration.

> SEBASTIAN
> [To Costa] Ah Jesus... What can I do?

> COSTA
> Nothing.

Costa places a sympathetic hand on Sebastián's knee.

> COSTA (CONT'D)
> Come on... next scene.

He walks off leaving Sebastián alone.

## 27. EXT. SET, CAMP – LATE AFTERNOON

End of the shoot for the day. The crew gather stuff together: props, clothes, electrical material – all being placed in different trucks. Some of the production cars start heading off in convoy.

The camera van is open and the driver and his assistant have a brief chat by the front of the vehicle.

Two Bolivian lads, young teenagers, prowl around.

They seize the opportunity. They grab what they can from the camera van: metallic camera cases, tripods, but worst of all, cans of film for the laboratory, piled one on top of the other beside the open door.

The lads quickly hide everything in an old cart and pop a plastic sheet over it and off they go.

## 28. INT. CORRIDOR AND SEBASTIAN'S ROOM – SAME NIGHT

Costa strides along a corridor. He knocks at Sebastián's door. An exhausted Sebastián answers.

> SEBASTIAN
> Anything? [Costa just shakes his head]… The rushes?

> COSTA
> The police just laughed…

> SEBASTIAN
> Fucking ignoramuses!… Thrown in a bin somewhere to rot!

> COSTA
> We can use second unit camera till we get replacements in three days… Insurers are going crazy and getting very nervous… Got a meeting with the District Governor about more security… need to lick his arse first at a reception…

SEBASTIAN
I want armed guards… shoot the fuckers next time!

COSTA
[Handing him some sheets of paper] New schedule… see what you think… you choose, but we have to cut Seb… the only way…

His eyes flash through the schedule.

SEBASTIAN
My slave scene?

COSTA
Three hundred extras!… Can't have that and the re-shoot…

SEBASTIAN
Put it back in!

COSTA
Well cut something else then!

SEBASTIAN
No. I'll put my salary against it…

COSTA
Jesus Seb… you can't do that!

SEBASTIAN
Do it!

COSTA
You could be left with nothing…

SEBASTIAN
Don't give a fuck! My money… put it back in.

A moment between them.

COSTA
Got to cut the extras too… for the rest of the shoot…

SEBASTIAN
Can we pay them less and bring in more?

Costa looks at him, amazed.

COSTA
I'll do my best…

SEBASTIAN
[With increasing frustration] Lost the drowning scene and at least five more… the film's falling apart… try to talk to them… make them understand what's at stake…

COSTA
For us… or for them?

SEBASTIAN
[Snapping] Don't play phoney progressive crap with me you cynical bastard! I know you…

COSTA
And that's why you got me down here… to do the dirty work.

Sebastián's mobile rings. His face drops as he realises who it is. Costa leaves, while Sebastián takes the call and shuts the door. He listens quietly for some time, his face showing signs of great stress.

SEBASTIAN
[Almost whispering] Christ Rose… I'm overwhelmed… you've no idea… [Pause] I don't want to be a stranger to a child… better to be a good dad later than a useless one now… We're still young… let's try and be more [struggling for word] objective.

ROSE
Try telling my breasts that… have a mind of their own.

Silence.

ROSE (CONT'D)
Well?

SEBASTIAN
It's [pause] against the tide...

ROSE
You're not writing a screenplay... speak your fucking mind!

SEBASTIAN
Okay. [Pause] I don't want to go ahead.

ROSE
With what Sebastián? Say it!

SEBASTIAN
With the pregnancy! Fuck! There, I said it... and didn't turn to dust!

Silence.

ROSE
[Quiet] I knew it. [Pause] I've already made an appointment at the clinic.

The line goes dead.

SEBASTIAN
Rose...

29. EXT. TOWN SQUARE – DAY

A mad scramble as Costa, Sebastián, Anton, Juan, Alberto, the assistant and several other members of the cast and crew make their way through an energetic demonstration in the town square on their way towards the Town Hall.

Water activists [a noisy group of water carriers, cocaleros, students and urban dwellers] hand out leaflets and several take one, including Anton. Again, the police are in the background.

Daniel is there with Enrique once again. As he spots him, Sebastián is taken aback.

> SEBASTIAN
> What the hell is he doing there?

> COSTA
> What can I do?... Lock him up?

As they enter the grandiose building Sebastián can see the District Governor, the mayor and top-brass military [alongside the local media] waiting to receive them at the top of the stairs.

> SEBASTIAN
> [Whispering to Costa] Arseholes...

> COSTA
> Smile you prick.

## 30. INT. TOWN HALL – DAY

Flash of a camera at top of the stairs. A beaming Sebastián smiles beside the DISTRICT GOVERNOR.

[The District Governor, the Mayor, politicians and various 'local worthies' host a reception for the film-makers. All the politicians and businessmen are dressed in Western suits, and not one of them has Indian features. Many look distinctively European, especially those with round-rimmed glasses and trimmed, grey beards.]

The Governor and his team shake hands and pose with the film-makers as the cameras still flash. The Governor makes a special attempt to get Anton, the best known, by his side.

RECEPTION: A main reception room, with old wooden furniture and conservative paintings on the wall... Businessmen and their wives, specially dressed for the occasion, and the odd priest and bishop mingle with the film-makers.

> DISTRICT GOVERNOR
> [To Anton] A great pleasure to meet you in the flesh...

> ANTON
> [Grabbing another glass of champagne from a passing waiter] I'm sure it is...

Sebastián and Costa glance at him nervously as he's already well over the limit.

> DISTRICT GOVERNOR
> Seen all your films. Every one…
>
> ANTON
> What a waste of time…

More nervous glances.

> DISTRICT GOVERNOR
> We are honoured to have you in our city… and doubly honoured to have you mention Bartolomé de las Casas… greatly underestimated in my view…
>
> SEBASTIAN
> [Glancing at Costa and co, impressed and surprised] Thank you… extra police have made all the difference… we feel much safer…
>
> DISTRICT GOVERNOR
> Any luck with the missing film?
>
> SEBASTIAN
> [Shakes his head] No, but we're still hopeful…

Loud yells. The excitement grows outside. A pall of smoke winding its way upwards becomes visible from the window overlooking the square. An assistant moves towards the irritated Governor and whispers into his ear.

> ASSISTANT
> They're burning the water bills…
>
> DISTRICT GOVERNOR
> [Whispering] Close the shutters… turn up the music.

More noise from the chaos outside.

> DISTRICT GOVERNOR (CONT'D)
> A little local difficulty… nothing to get excited about…

                   ANTON
    ...If there's enough champagne!... 'Let them eat
    cake'!

Sebastián fights back a chuckle. He enjoys the reference but has to keep a straight face.

                DISTRICT GOVERNOR
    It's only an excuse for some hotheads to stir up
    hatred amongst the desperate and gain a name
    for themselves...

Police sirens screech in the square. Nervous faces among the guests. Sebastián and Costa glance at the shutters being closed over by staff. The classical music in the background is turned up.

                  SEBASTIAN
    If you don't mind me saying... I do have a little
    sympathy for them...

                   ANTON
    That's my boy!

                DISTRICT GOVERNOR
    Perhaps if you were better informed... We are a
    small country with limited resources... we can
    only provide a first-class water system with major
    investment from overseas... The problem with
    the poor... not to blame them... is they think
    government money grows on trees... the simple
    concept of inflation is beyond them...

Loud bangs of tear gas canisters being fired.

                DISTRICT GOVERNOR (CONT'D)
    ...given the history of exploitation Indian distrust
    is embedded in their genes... difficult to reason
    with the illiterate... we have objective reports
    from Harvard professors, the IMF, the World
    Bank...

ANTON
I'd like to see those wankers manage a family on forty dollars a month!

Embarrassed looks all round, but the Governor sails on regardless after a cursory glance at him.

DISTRICT GOVERNOR
…The entire globe deregulates, international treaties are signed with the WTO… consumers demand efficiency…

ANTON
And 'transparency' my good man! Cayman Islands?… [Holding up the leaflet he got from outside] Who heard of sixteen per cent profit… by contract! [To Governor, winking] A little back-hander eh?!…

Costa buries his face in his hands and whispers to Maria beside him.

COSTA
Get that fuck-wit out of here!

DISTRICT GOVERNOR
…And here… they burn their bills and hurl rocks at the police… the cult of victim versus modernity… I'm embarrassed by their backwardness…

SEBASTIAN
[Polite] Someone on two dollars a day… can't pay a 300 per cent increase in a water bill… [Smiling] At least that's what I heard…

DISTRICT GOVERNOR
[Smiling] Funny… that's what I heard you were paying the extras…

Sebastián is stunned and embarrassed.

SEBASTIAN
We have a very tight budget…

                    DISTRICT GOVERNOR
        Haven't we all...

Maria manages to grab Anton and lead him out of harm's way towards the waiters. Costa moves closer to the Governor.

                    COSTA
        My apologies... he's highly talented... highly
        strung... and drinks too much.

The Governor appreciates Costa's words. There is an intelligence and curiosity to the man.

The noise outside is getting greater. More bangs and screaming from demonstrators.

                    COSTA (CONT'D)
        I'll be honest... We're very concerned about the
        rumours... [The Governor raises his eyebrows as
        if mystified]... the water dispute might get out
        of hand... and stop us filming... Anything you
        can do?

Tension grows outside as more sirens blare.

                    DISTRICT GOVERNOR
        [Politely smiling] If we give one inch... these
        dumb brutes will drag us back to the Stone
        Age...

Costa looks at him, and can sense his ruthlessness.

Sudden crescendo of whistling and shouts from outside.

## 31. INT. COSTA'S 4 X 4, ROAD TO DANIEL'S HOUSE – NIGHT

Costa drives his big 4 x 4 though the town.

Sebastián is in the passenger seat and highly agitated. They are midway though an emergency phone call, on an open speaker.

The caller speaks with great urgency.

> INSURER
>
> [English] …crystal fucking clear brothers…
> insurance does not cover state of war or anything
> pertaining thereto, civil or political strife of any
> sort, coup d'état, revolution or invasion from
> whatever source…
>
> COSTA
>
> From cockroaches to aliens…
>
> INSURER
>
> 'Correcto'… My advice is pack up and get the
> fuck out of there… Pronto!
>
> SEBASTIAN
>
> …to a fucking studio?!
>
> COSTA
>
> It won't work! You've seen the rushes!
>
> INSURER
>
> Your choice… you guys could lose the lot… be
> warned.

Receiver goes dead. Sebastián pounds the dashboard. They pull up outside Daniel's house. Sebastián has a word with an assistant who's smoking outside Daniel's home.

> SEBASTIAN
>
> Any broken bones?
>
> ASSISTANT
>
> Just severe bruising…
>
> SEBASTIAN
>
> His face?
>
> ASSISTANT
>
> We'll get away with it… just…
>
> SEBASTIAN
>
> [To Costa, intense] Make the fucker
> understand… Get him to do the cross scene and
> we have a chance… if not, we're done for.

Costa jumps out of the vehicle. Sebastián, increasingly on edge, slips into the driver's seat and drives off at a perilous speed.

## 32. EXT. INSIDE DANIEL'S KITCHEN – NIGHT

A shirtless Daniel sits back to front on a chair. His wife Teresa tenderly rubs ointment on ugly gashes and bruises on his back after a beating from the police. His face is also badly bruised and swollen.

Belen, sitting on a bench in the corner, looks at Costa. Costa is seething.

> COSTA
> …What the fuck's the matter with you Daniel? Do you know the time and effort we've put in trying to get this film off the ground? How many people are behind this, the money we're risking? If you get fucked… we get fucked!… Are you the only bodyguard in the city?

Daniel winces as a deep wound is cleaned.

> COSTA (CONT'D)
> Just three weeks to go… is that too much to ask?

Costa is infuriated by Daniel's silence.

> COSTA (CONT'D)
> Ahh! The big-quiet-silent-dignified-Indian… *One Flew Over the Cuckoo's Nest*… is that it? [Still nothing] We catch you at one more demonstration and you don't get paid a fucking cent… do you hear me?

Still nothing. Belen's eyes flash in anger. Silence. Daniel doesn't bat an eyelid.

> COSTA (CONT'D)
> I have a proposal for you…

Costa takes out a thick wad of US dollars and smacks them down on the table.

> COSTA (CONT'D)
> We'll give you a 10,000 dollar bonus… IF you give up the water demonstrations till all your scenes are done…

Again more silence. Belen stares at the pile of cash.

> COSTA (CONT'D)
> Below you… or not enough?

Still nothing.

> COSTA (CONT'D)
> [Pointing at the money] Half now… half at the end… [Still no answer. Growing frustration.] This is your last chance to get out of this shit-hole and you're smart enough to know it!

Belen listens, hurt. She gets up and leaves. Costa watches her make her way out then turns to Daniel and his wife.

> DANIEL
> Think you can buy everything… don't you?

Costa is about to grab the money again.

> DANIEL (CONT'D)
> Okay.

Costa is stunned, but reacts quickly.

> COSTA
> No more demonstrations! You do exactly what we say till the shoot is finished… Do I have your word?

Daniel nods. The three look at each other. Costa leaves.

Daniel walks painstakingly towards the table, picks up the money, and then looks at it.

He hands it to his wife.

33. INT. HOTEL LOBBY – EARLY MORNING

Busy hotel lobby; great concern on the faces of the waiting crew who look closely at the second and third assistant directors as they whisper nervously among themselves. The third is agitated and obviously stressed. Costa approaches them with concern.

> COSTA
> Where is he?

> ASSISTANT
> In his room, but no answer… [Lowering his
> voice]… He was wandering about the gardens at
> 4am! I'm really worried Costa… he looked
> terrible yesterday after he lost his rag…

34. INT. CORRIDOR AND SEBASTIAN'S ROOM – EARLY MORNING

A duty manager lets Costa into Sebastián's room. Costa walks in. He's shocked. Open books and sketches are strewn all over the floor. Sebastián lies on the sofa, wide awake, staring up at the ceiling. He looks ghostly pale, totally bereft of energy. His eyes barely flicker.

> COSTA
> Never slept a wink the whole night… and
> throwing up as well?

He doesn't respond. Costa glances round at the chaos.

> COSTA (CONT'D)
> The only way to shut down that fucking brain
> of yours is a lobotomy…

There is a hint of life in Sebastián's eyes.

> SEBASTIAN
> [Whispered] I'm cracking up…

Costa sits down on the sofa beside him.

                    COSTA
[Tender] Knew that seven years ago... you
phoned me up at 2am!... Remember?... Listen
to this Costa!... From a priest called
Montesinos!... Sixteenth century!... Talking over
me in a babble... 'No it can't wait Costa!' [Pause]
I was just about to screw that little blond from
the bar... Couldn't get you off the fucking
phone... [Pause, and a hint of a smile from
Sebastián]... 'From a humble straw church' you
said... 'one man against an empire... a voice in
the desert... [Pause, whisper]... Are these not
men?

                  SEBASTIAN
'...Do they not have rational souls...?'

                  TOGETHER
'Are you not obliged to love them as
yourselves...?'

                    COSTA
That's what really got you! [Glancing at the chaos
around him] Why you suffered all this... You
never give in Sebastián... [with total conviction]
Not now... not ever... Come on...

Costa grabs him up by the arm. Sebastián's face... looking up to him...

## 35. INT. QUEEN'S BEDROOM, SPAIN – DAY (16TH CENT.)

Now the face of Queen Isabella, ghostly pale, but still stunningly beautiful, as she lies back on a bed.

Bartolomé bends over and whispers intimately into the Queen's ear. The Queen listens to him, barely able to talk. Montesinos sits on the other side of the bed, paying close attention. The royal physician loiters in the background, while two Royal advisors, [unimpressed and cynical] study proceedings from their position by the window hardly able to conceal their contempt.

#### BARTOLOME
[Gently, but forcefully]... Indians have a different language, Your Majesty, but it is just as complex... they also possess the most delicate art... Look at these... [he pulls out little statues, beads and drawings which he lays down for her to see]... and their history is passed on by song in intricate patterns... at first sight it seems mysterious... and it is, but underneath... [glancing at the advisors]... they're just like us... what we feel, they feel... they are tender, sensitive, intelligent and contradictory! They laugh and cry just like we do... I have intimate personal experience of their humanity...

Bartolomé catches sight of the advisors smirking.

#### MONTESINOS
They are human beings, Your Majesty, with full human faculties, and as such therefore have certain inalienable natural rights...

#### QUEEN ISABELLA
Many jurists and professors disagree!

Advisors nod their approval.

#### BARTOLOME
Your Majesty...

She cuts Bartolomé off and gestures to Montesinos to continue.

#### MONTESINOS
They have natural rights which are undermined by a system of virtual slavery.

#### QUEEN ISABELLA
What is the solution then?

#### MONTESINOS
Dismantle Indian grants to Spanish settlers and put an end to further conquests immediately.

The advisors loudly scoff.

>    QUEEN ISABELLA
>    [Trying to sit up] There'll be uproar... we can't
>    have that!

>    BARTOLOME
>    Better uproar than they burn in hell for all
>    eternity.

Stunned silence from them all and even Montesinos is taken aback. The Queen's eyes flash at Bartolomé. He stares back at her. The physician, shocked, approaches.

Costa, in a dark corner of the set, follows the scene closely. He watches Sebastián, beside the camera, who follows every beat like an excited child.

>    QUEEN ISABELLA
>    [In a slow, severe tone] I would remind you,
>    Father, I have obligations to the conquistadors.
>    Men who have shed their blood and invested
>    their own private wealth to gain Spain a
>    continent!

>    BARTOLOME
>    By what means Your Majesty? The torture,
>    murder, and enslavement of Indian communities
>    that would defy the Royal imagination...

>    QUEEN ISABELLA
>    What about the laws of Burgos? We passed them
>    to protect the Indians.

>    MONTESINOS
>    Imprecise and ignored. We must replace corrupt
>    Royal officials here and in the Indies who get
>    rich at your expense, treat the Indians like brute
>    animals and do nothing but implement the
>    wishes of these tyrants that call themselves
>    Christians...

A filthy look from the physician and incensed advisors. Bartolomé can see the Queen is fading and he glances at Montesinos.

> PHYSICIAN
> I think that's all we have time for.

The Queen looks over at her advisors.

> QUEEN ISABELLA
> Gentlemen… what do you say to our friends?

> ADVISOR 1
> Perhaps we should beg all Spaniards to pack their bags, sail back home, and leave the way free for the Portuguese.

> ADVISOR 2
> It's about time we dismantled the entire economy, and sabotaged commerce between two continents…

> ADVISOR 1
> [Chuckling] Most entertaining…

> BARTOLOME
> …if you find mutilation entertaining…

> ADVISOR 1
> You make enemies very quickly Padre…

> MONTESINOS
> Not as quickly as your business associates murder children… How much are they paying you?

The advisor's cheeks redden.

> PHYSICIAN
> Gentlemen! Her Majesty is not well and must rest!

> BARTOLOME
> May God grant you a speedy recovery so you can give this matter, of critical importance to the Royal Conscience, your personal attention!

The royal physician is aghast at his affront to Royalty.

> QUEEN ISABELLA
> Are you trying to frighten me Padre?

> BARTOLOME
> I'm telling you the truth.

They look at each other for a moment.

## 36. INT. SEAMLESS CONTINUATION OF PREVIOUS SCENE

Pull back to see the entire sixteenth-century set and crew behind. Sebastián nods at the actors.

> SEBASTIAN
> [Quiet, to respect the atmosphere] Very good… excellent… maybe a *fraction* faster next time…

Costa, who's watching Sebastián from a distance, looks at him and gives the thumbs up. Sebastián, touched, appreciates the gesture and gives the thumbs up too. A moment between them, and then he's back studying the script.

## 37. INT. COSTA'S ROOM IN HOTEL – NIGHT

Costa, on top, dwarfs the petite body of Wendy, the prostitute. Her eyes are closed, her face turned away and her delicate neck stretched out as Costa pounds her. As he is about to come he whispers gently.

> COSTA
> Open your eyes. Open them. Now. I want to see you…

She does so. A few long moments of quivering release.

As Costa relieves himself he pathetically strokes her cheek as he looks into her dark child-like eyes and can feel the guilt already sweep over him.

LATER:

A naked Costa slouches on the bed as he watches Wendy put her clothes back on, covering her small body. She winces slightly as she bends to put on her pants.

>COSTA (CONT'D)
>What's wrong?

She shakes her head.

>COSTA (CONT'D)
>Did I hurt you?

She shakes her head again.

>WENDY
>[Pause] Do you want me to stay the night?

>COSTA
>How old are you Wendy?

>WENDY
>Told you... nineteen...

>COSTA
>Please. Tell me the truth.

She ignores him. She finishes dressing and then goes over to Costa who gives her cash from his wallet. After paying her his due he hesitates, and then gives her a big fat tip. Her eyes flash at the cash and then she looks at him.

>WENDY
>You don't want to see me again... do you?

Costa looks ashamed.

>COSTA
>I don't know Wendy.

They look at each other for a moment. She heads for the door. As she leaves, without looking back at him, she whispers something.

>WENDY
>Sixteen...

The door clicks shut. Costa leans his head back against the wall.

38. EXT. BY A COMMUNITY WELL – DAY

Dusty marginal barrio.

A group of a dozen police protect two tradesmen [wearing water company uniforms] who put a steel cover and heavy padlock on a community well as women and children hurl fierce abuse at them in Quechua and Aymara. [Along following lines.]

>                    WOMEN'S VOICES
>           We dug this well with our hands you bastards!...
>           Get out of here... What will the children
>           drink... dirty truck water?

Several of the women attack the police with the first thing they can put their hands on. Some are hurled to the ground as the police pull out their batons to defend themselves.

39. EXT. FILM LOCATION, HILL IN COUNTRYSIDE – DAY

Impressive hillside location.

Sebastián, in preparation for an enormous scene, is in full flight and active discussion with his team. Some three dozen heavily armed Spanish settlers take the odd drag of a cigarette as they hang around waiting for the shoot to begin.

The art department put the final touches to thirteen rough wooden crosses that have been erected in stunning surrounds. Around the bottom of each, logs and crisp branches are ready for the torch.

A Spanish actor playing a Franciscan priest chats to the actor playing the Commander, and Las Casas.

In the distance all does not look well. Sebastián is stressed, and even from a distance they can hear his shouts.

BY THE CROSS: A worried crew surround Sebastián who has grabbed one of the phones.

                        SEBASTIAN
                Where the fuck are my Indians?!

40. EXT. MAIN CROSSROAD IN CENTRE OF
COCHABAMBA – DAY

High tension at crossroads in the town centre.

Costa is in the middle of it all, a phone stuck to his ear.

                        SEBASTIAN'S VOICE
                ...If you don't get Daniel up here now Costa I'll
                burn the cunt for real! I mean it. I don't care
                about their fucking plumbing. Get him here
                right now!

Heavily armoured riot police, in a high state of alert, surround some two hundred or so Indians who block a major intersection into the city.

There are honking cars and police sirens in the background.

The media wade their way towards the Indian leaders, including Enrique, with Daniel at his side. [Daniel co-ordinates security and a team of a dozen or so strongly built young Indians, arms linked together, determined to protect them.]

Both Daniel and leaders are inside the circle.

Costa fights to the front and is next to the chain of young Indians who will not let him though to speak to Daniel. Costa shouts as best he can above the chaos.

                        COSTA
                [Fierce] Daniel! You promised us! Don't fuck
                with me!... Get into the Jeep right now!...
                Entire crew are waiting for you... this is the most
                important scene in the film!

Daniel glances at him but he's more concerned with the protective circle and the police around them.

COSTA (CONT'D)
Daniel... you lying bastard! Move it!

The police begin to shove more aggressively. More and more pressure on the circle. Costa catches sight of more riot police arriving armed with guns and rubber bullets.

COSTA (CONT'D)
Fuck!... You're going to get hurt!

DANIEL
[Snapping] Fuck off!

Enrique, just behind Daniel, grabs the loudspeaker. Costa catches sight of even more police arriving.

ENRIQUE
[Shouting above the chaos] After extensive consultation with urban dwellers, field workers, students, churches and the trade unions... we the people of Cochabamba hereby give notice that if the water privatisation contract is not repealed within forty-eight hours we will begin an indefinite blockade of the entire city!... [Shock on Costa's face] The water is ours!... We will not allow it to be stolen by foreign shareholders who sit by their pools while our children die of thirst...

The police, armed with batons and shields, charge. A full frontal attack! The demonstrators fight back as best as they can with their fists and their feet.

A snatch squad of riot police fiercely fight their way towards the Indian leaders. A round of rubber bullets is fired at close quarters. Terrible screams. Some fall injured.

Costa is terrified by the violence.

COSTA
Jesus Christ...

Screaming and cursing.

Costa cowers, but he too is knocked over in the chaos. In the distance he sees Daniel fight and kick several police who try to arrest Enrique.

Shrieking, cursing and another deafening volley of rubber bullets among the chaos as Costa dives for cover.

41. INT. FIVE-STAR HOTEL – EVENING

Sober atmosphere as Costa, Sebastián, Alberto, Juan, Anton, Maria and a few more from the crew are captivated by evening news film footage under an enormous TV screen.

[Real footage from April 2000 gives a sense of the enormous scale of the growing dispute.]

A flash of Enrique [with Daniel part of the circle protecting him] making the blockade ultimatum followed by the charge.

Random acts of violence.

A protester on the ground is severely beaten and kicked till he lies motionless. There are sounds of shock from those watching as he is pounded by a rifle butt.

#### ALBERTO
Jesus… I can't stand it!

Next: Image of Daniel and others dragged off and thrown into a police vehicle.

#### MARIA
There's Daniel!

#### JUAN
Poor bastards… will be beaten to a pulp…

#### SEBASTIAN
Stupid fucker!… They'll lock him up and throw away the key…

The actors are stunned by his reaction. Sebastián catches Anton staring at him.

SEBASTIAN (CONT'D)
What are you staring at you drunken prick!

Sebastián bounds off to the bar, followed by Costa. Anton, Juan and Alberto watch him march off.

ANTON
[Reflective, with respect, to a shocked Juan and Alberto] I admire the boy…

BY SEBASTIAN AND COSTA: Sebastián looks furious. From a distance, more riot scenes on TV.

SEBASTIAN
Nothing works without this scene… nothing! These blockades can last for weeks… fuckers!

He's bursting with tension; a wildness in him.

SEBASTIAN (CONT'D)
I won't give up now Costa…

Costa is dialling a number as he stares at Sebastián.

COSTA
[On phone] Costa here Puri… [Pause]… How much cash can you get your hands on tonight?

Sebastián stares at him.

COSTA (CONT'D)
Ten grand. Okay. Find out where they are holding Daniel… get the name of the police chief… set up a meeting… now. I said now! Phone production… we're doing the cross scene tomorrow… after that I don't give a fuck… Yes you heard me right… move it.

SEBASTIAN
You're insane…

COSTA
We're not out yet…

## 42. INT. POLICE STATION – NIGHT

Costa and Sebastián are escorted along a shabby corridor towards the police chief's office. As they pass a noisy changing room Sebastián stops for a moment; muscular young riot police, some still with protective gear, others half-dressed or plain naked, prance around like teenagers. They are joking and laughing. Some flick each other with towels and they let off steam after the riot. They catch sight of him staring, and the door is slammed shut in his face as the crescendo of noise grows inside.

INSIDE OFFICE: Costa and Sebastián sit opposite the POLICE CHIEF. He has intelligent eyes and a lean military look. Costa lays down a thick wad of dollar bills wrapped up in an elastic band.

> COSTA
> We need him to finish the film. [Indicating] Ten grand.

A long moment between them. The chief's eyes flick towards the cash.

> CHIEF
> On one condition.

Sebastián and Costa's eyes light up.

> CHIEF (CONT'D)
> We get him back straight after the scene. He's a nasty fucker… ex-military.

Sebastián recoils at the idea.

Silence.

> SEBASTIAN
> I can't do that.

Costa looks at Sebastián.

> COSTA
> Can we have a moment please…

Costa and Sebastián move from the office into the grubby corridor.

CORRIDOR: They speak in sharp whispers, face to face. [Still the distant sound of chanting police.]

> SEBASTIAN
> What if he's beaten up... tortured... disappeared... Christ Almighty! Anything could happen! I won't have it on my conscience...

> COSTA
> He's in prison now! We didn't put him there! And the bastard ripped us off! [Pause] Without this scene we're fucked... and you know it.

> SEBASTIAN
> Jesus...

Long pause. Costa holds his eye.

> COSTA
> I say we do it.

> SEBASTIAN
> We've got to tell him...

> COSTA
> Okay... after the scene is done... or he'll be off like a shot.

> SEBASTIAN
> I can't cope with this...

> COSTA
> Yes. You can.

Sebastián squirms. And then relinquishes.

> COSTA (CONT'D)
> [Holding his eye] Good...

CELL IN POLICE STATION: Costa enters Daniel's cell. He's had another beating.

> COSTA (CONT'D)
> You promised me… gave your word… you lied to me.

> DANIEL
> No water. No life. You lot don't understand.

A long moment between them. At last Costa flicks his eyes to the open door of the cell. Daniel rises to his feet with great difficulty.

Daniel makes his way out as Costa stares at him.

## 43. EXT. 4 X 4 STREET TO DANIEL'S HOME – NIGHT

Costa, Sebastián and Daniel in the 4 x 4 in total silence. They drive towards Daniel's home and stop outside.

Teresa rushes out. She is relieved to see Daniel, but worried by his appearance. Daniel, his clothes ripped and filthy after the riot and arrest, pulls himself from the vehicle. He moves over to Sebastián by the open passenger window and stares at him and then Costa. He lays his hand on Sebastián's arm.

> DANIEL
> Thank you.

Sebastián makes to speak but then freezes. The moment is gone. Daniel limps inside towards his home, helped by Teresa.

Sebastián pounds the dashboard in front of him.

> SEBASTIAN
> Fuck!

## 44. EXT. HILLS WITH CROSSES – DAY (16TH CENTURY)

Hundreds of INDIANS have been forced to assemble around the crosses. Hatuey, although tied at the neck with another twenty or so Indians, stares at his captors in defiance.

The terrified Indians are pushed closer. The COMMANDER and his CAPTAIN organise proceedings. Bartolomé desperately pursues the Commander as the latter, ignoring him, barks orders.

> COMMANDER
> I want everyone here… women and children…

> BARTOLOME
> In the name of Christ! I beg you! [The
> Commander ignores him]… This will turn every
> Indian against us for generations! The Crown will
> prosecute you!

> COMMANDER
> I don't think so…

> BARTOLOME
> What about the teachings of the Church?!

The commander reaches the SOLDIERS guarding the prisoners. Hatuey stares at them.

> COMMANDER
> [To Captain] Pick out thirteen, and let the rest
> go free. [To Bartolomé] One for each Disciple…
> and one for Christ himself! Want to choose them
> Padre?

The soldiers start laughing.

> BARTOLOME
> This is a sacrilege!

> COMMANDER
> No! An example! [Indicating a Franciscan friar]
> Join the Franciscan… save their souls… if they
> have any. [To soldier] If he interferes, arrest him.

The Captain approaches the Indians.

> CAPTAIN
> The evangelists...

The soldiers start joking as the Captain picks them out at random, pointing to one, and then switching, at the last moment, for the entertainment of the soldiers who cut the specified Indian free and lead him to a cross.

> CAPTAIN (CONT'D)
> [Pointing] Matthew... Mark... Luke... and John!

Hatuey stands quiet and erect as his friends are led off and tied to the crosses.

> CAPTAIN (CONT'D)
> Padre... help me... I've forgotten the names...

The soldiers join the fun and start shouting out names, often incorrectly, while insulting the chosen Indian. Bartolomé stands in shock as he hears sacred names taken in vain. Sick at heart he turns to look at the Indians being gathered to witness the spectacle. Young and old. His eyes skip from FACE TO FACE; some old and burnt from the sun, and others fresh. Though passive, underneath he can sense their terror. Children grip on to parents as they are herded along towards the crosses and pass Hatuey and other Indians tied at the neck.

> CAPTAIN (CONT'D)
> Now! Who gets to play Christ?

He moves forward to Hatuey who stares at him in defiance. The Commander nods his agreement. Hatuey is cut free from an ADOLESCENT who grips on to him. Hatuey hugs him and then rubs his face to his cheek.

> ADOLESCENT
> [Whisper] I swear... I'll fight them till the day I die.

Hatuey is pulled from him and led to the middle cross, as the other ten Indians are cut free.

A young soldier approaches with a lit torch.

As Hatuey is tied to the cross the FRANCISCAN approaches with an Indian TRANSLATOR who translates simultaneously. Bartolomé moves closer too.

> FRANCISCAN
> [Holding up a small cross] In the name of Christ you can still save your soul… you must understand the difference between heaven and hell… ask Our Lord for forgiveness, I'll baptise you, and you will have glory and eternal peace in heaven… if not, you will suffer eternal torment in hell… [To translator] Does he understand?

> HATUEY
> [Translated] Do Christians go to heaven?

> FRANCISCAN
> [Translated] The good ones do…

> HATUEY
> [Translated] Let me go to Hell!

Hatuey kicks the cross flying from the priest's hand. Soldiers curse and roughly tie his legs to the cross. The Commander, turning to the assembled crowd, calls for silence and his words are translated again by the same Indian.

> COMMANDER
> Remember… this is what happens if you defy the Christians!

He raises his hand. Two adult Indians restrain the same adolescent as he tries to run towards Hatuey. Two soldiers, one at each end, run from one pyre to the next lighting the bushes underneath the crosses. Hatuey shouts out in his own tongue, like a mantra, that is taken up by the others tied to the cross. Sense of defiance, above the terror. It communicates to the Indian crowd; sudden sense of danger and fury. The Commander notices, as does Bartolomé. The soldiers meet in the middle and both set fire to Hatuey's pyre.

Bartolomé, opposite Hatuey, sees his defiant face contort in agony as the flames lick his legs. Still he screams, as the others join in.

Bartolomé grabs the Indian translator beside him.

>BARTOLOME
>What's he saying?

The Indian stares in wonder at Hatuey.

>TRANSLATOR
>'I despise you, your God and your greed!'

>BARTOLOME
>May God forgive us.

There is a murmur and a wave of emotion among the Indians forced to watch as they step forward; Panuca among them. They begin to chant a single word.

>INDIANS
>Hatuey! Hatuey! Hatuey! Hatuey!

The soldiers become increasingly nervous. Some are spooked at the show of defiance.

>COMMANDER
>[To Bartolomé] What the hell are they saying?

The chant grows stronger.

>BARTOLOME
>His name... thanks to you, never to be
>forgotten...

Crackle of dry timber, roaring fire, and now the screaming name. Hatuey's face melts behind smoke and flame. Held for a long long moment.

>SEBASTIAN
>Cut! [Anxious, to director of photography]
>Okay?

He smiles and nods. In the distance, at strategic points, two other camera units give the thumbs up.

There is a loud cheer from the crew. Sebastián punches the air in triumph and approaches Costa.

SEBASTIAN [CONT'D)
You fucking did it Costa. [Pause] I love you man.

He holds Costa in a warm embrace.

COSTA
[Real conviction] We're going to do it!

A moment between them.

They hear a commotion and look round towards it.

A DOZEN POLICEMEN sprint through the set.

Daniel, covered in smoke, is surrounded by them. They drag Daniel to a police van, but more and more of the Indian cast from scene just completely surround them.

Fury!

[Sudden escalation, which seems totally surreal, as twenty-first-century uniformed policemen are accosted by sixteenth-century Indians; as if wrath from witnesses in the scene just completed is transferred to the present.]

They struggle into one of the two police vans but more Indians crowd around the vehicle and begin to pound the sides and windscreens. Now they begin to rock the vehicle back and forward. It bounces dangerously. There is no stopping them now despite pleas for calm. The vehicle is overturned.

Costa and Sebastián sprint towards the trouble.

The back door is hurled open and the terrified policemen inside pull out guns from holsters and point them nervously.

Terrible moment of tension and danger.

Shouts and insults in Aymara and Quechua which Costa can't understand.

COSTA [CONT'D)
Everyone… calm down!

> POLCEMAN
> [Screaming] Get back or we'll shoot! Get back!

Despite pointed guns the Indians move forward and grab Daniel and pull him from the vehicle. Daniel disappears through the crowd as Costa tries to calm the terrified police who nervously emerge from the back of the overturned vehicle.

Sebastián approaches Costa. The Indians taunt the police despite the guns.

> SEBASTIAN
> Christ… feels like a dream…

## 45. EXT. COMMUNITY CENTRE, POPULAR BARRIO – NIGHT

Sense of chaos and high tension. Costa, along with Maria, is desperate to find out what is going on.

[Include real participants of the Cochabamba water wars. The language used should be what feels right to each speaker, with Aymara and Quechua dominating, though there might be some Spanish. Sense of ordinary people, ordinary faces; men and women. Contradictory points of view are presented. Some are nervous and speak too quietly, while others are sharp and to the point. Some fear excessive police violence, while others are sure the army will intervene and use this as an excuse to imprison or kill community leaders. Snippets of many points of view. It all makes a strong impression on Costa who is agitated too by the rumours.]

> ENRIQUE
> Can I have your attention please… silence please!… The proposal before us… discussed in barrios all round the city… is that we take the Plaza and then Water HQ [loud cheers] and occupy these until the water is returned into our hands…

> MAN 2
> That's exactly what they want… an excuse for a bloodbath!

#### ENRIQUE
Everyone gets a chance to give their views... everyone!

[Some of the contributions might be along the following lines.]

#### WOMAN
...I'm very very scared... who knows what can happen?

#### MAN 1
'A few thirsty peasants... lost in the Andes'... that's what the papers call us... they insult us... 'backward', 'stupid' and worse...

#### OLD WOMAN 1
[Emotional] Air and water... that's all we've got left! Sacred... Life is water and water is life!... Look at these hands [tough from work] that's all I've got... how can they take water from me?

#### WOMAN 2
How can I pay four hundred and fifty dollars a year?! Might as well shoot us and be done with...

#### WOMAN 3
...and that's exactly what they'll do!... How many miners did they shoot last time?

Costa is increasingly worried.

#### COSTA
[To Maria] Fucking nightmare... we're screwed!

Someone runs to Daniel, slips him a piece of paper, and whispers to him in some agitation. It attracts Enrique's attention.

#### ENRIQUE
What is it?

                    DANIEL
        A state of siege has been announced!... Riot
        police backed by the army are on their way from
        the capital...

                    VOICES
        We'll have to block roads into the city! Now!

Costa is shocked. The man who came in with the news cannot contain himself.

                    INDIAN
        [Shouting] There is wild talk of a massacre...
        remember the factory workers shot in the
        Plaza... could happen again!

Loud shouts and discussions among everyone. Genuine fear. Costa rushes from the centre with mobile phone already at his ear.

## 46. EXT. STREET OUTSIDE MEETING – NIGHT

Costa is on the phone.

                    COSTA
        ...got to get out before we're trapped in the
        city!... Actors together... bags packed... I'll join
        you later.

Costa is stopped in his tracks as he notices Teresa, Daniel's wife, and other women piling stones into a small vegetable cart. An older woman struggles with her shawl which is full of stones too. Other women do the same with another old cart. Some adolescents, both boys and girls, are making rough sling-shots. He catches sight of Belen practicing; she skilfully places a stone in her sling and then lets fly. He moves towards her.

                    COSTA (CONT'D)
        What are you doing Belen?

                    TERESA
        [Swinging her sling] What else have we got?

Costa can't believe it.

COSTA

You're up against an army! Have you seen their weapons?

Teresa looks at him, in silence, and carries on piling stones. He stares at them with dismay and deep frustration.

Daniel approaches him.

DANIEL

Can you help us? Transport... walkie-talkies... anything?

COSTA

[Furious] This is insane Daniel... You'll be slaughtered! [Daniel looks at him, saying nothing.] I'm sorry... we've been instructed by our financiers to leave the city... I'm sorry... it's out of my hands...

Daniel looks at him for a long moment, almost with compassion.

DANIEL

It's always 'in' our hands. Always...

They look at each other for a moment. Costa catches sight of Belen who has been watching him for a while.

COSTA

I can't. I'm sorry.

Daniel leaves him. Costa stares at Belen and Teresa who go back to piling stones onto their clapped-out little cart.

COSTA (CONT'D)

[To himself] Fuck!

He heads to his 4 x 4.

47. INT. HOTEL – NIGHT

Feverish activity in the hotel lounge. Men in suits are agitated and demand information from harassed hotel workers. Nearly everyone is on a mobile phone. In a corner, Costa, Sebastián, actors Juan, Alberto and Anton and several others crowd around a TV set. [Their bags are packed and they are ready to go.]

[Again, REAL FOOTAGE to give a sense of scale.]

Images of soldiers running through the streets. They sing macho songs in rhythm with their thumping boots. They look keen for action. Deeply sinister and disconcerting as the hubbub in the office dies down.

More images: a team of police on enormous motorbikes revving up powerful engines.

### ALBERTO
Sorry guys… this is scary… I want a plane home. Tonight! I mean it.

### JUAN
Me too…

Costa and Sebastián stare at each other in shock.

### SEBASTIAN
We need you! We can't finish the film without you!

### COSTA
Come on guys… you can't just dump us… you have a contract signed…

### ALBERTO
Don't bullshit me with that when you can't guarantee our safety…

### COSTA
Yes I can… [Holding a map in his hand, indicating] We can drive there in about eight hours… landscape is more or less the same… and it's safe!

                    JUAN
A wife and two kids... [a glance at Alberto] I'm sorry...

                   ALBERTO
Anything could happen... we want out.

                    ANTON
[Staring at Juan and Alberto] Run little rabbits run run run!... Let's leave these poor Indian fuckers to their fate once again! Pair of yellow wankers... What would Bartolomé have done? [Slapping Alberto on the chest] Any life left in that useless heart?!

Juan and Alberto are stunned by his reaction.

                   ALBERTO
What the fuck can we do?

                    ANTON
[Real passion] Least we can do is move to a safe place and finish the work... we owe them that for Christ's sake! Come on!

They are stunned into silence. Costa spots his chance.

                    COSTA
[Striking the map in his hand, indicating] I swear it's safe... I spoke to people there fifteen minutes ago and I've hired private security...

                    ANTON
Let's go for it boys...

                    COSTA
We can pack up essentials overnight... and get the hell out before we're trapped inside the city...[Shouting over at an assistant at their desk] Are the roads still clear?

                  ASSISTANT
Yeah... for how long we don't know...

                        SEBASTIAN
            [Desperately to Juan and Alberto] I beg you…

                        ANTON
            I'm in…

Long pause. They confront Anton's staring eyes; almost mesmerising. Costa stares at Anton.

                        ANTON (CONT'D)
            Let's go for it.

Tension. At last.

                        ALBERTO
            Okay.

Juan reluctantly nods too.

                        SEBASTIAN
            [Quietly] Thank you… [To the entire office]
            Right guys… out of here!

They all get up and move off apart from Costa and Anton.

                        COSTA
            Thanks…

                        ANTON
            Don't. [Pause] It's my last film.

He stiffly pulls himself up and walks off.

48. INT. WAREHOUSE – MORNING

Costa is at the centre of pandemonium at the warehouse. Backs of several trucks are loaded up, doors slammed, and a man with a whistle waves them out in orderly fashion to guide them out into the street where they line up and wait to leave in convoy. Other vans, including one with the mastiffs, are loaded up with the last materials.

One of the assistants has a radio and there is a live report from the riots in the town centre. Sebastián and a few others cluster round. It sounds terrifying – sounds of screams, shouts, rocks and tear gas canisters.

An assistant, with a phone to his ear, shouts at Costa.

> ASSISTANT
> One road open and about to close... got to move now!

A concerned Sebastián joins Costa.

> COSTA
> [Shouting] That's it... lock them up... no more... dump the rest... we're on the move!

Costa suddenly sees Teresa, Belen's mother, by the warehouse door, looking at him. Costa and Sebastián go up to her.

> COSTA (CONT'D)
> What's wrong Teresa?

> TERESA
> Belen's hurt.

> COSTA
> Belen! Fuck! What happened?

> TERESA
> She was in the street...

> COSTA
> Doing what?!

> TERESA
> [Almost overcome] She ran off with her brothers... she wanted to help them... I told her to stay with me... but she didn't listen.

> COSTA
> Fucking hell!

> TERESA
> [Wiping tears away] She's been shot!

> SEBASTIAN
> Oh no!

TERESA
Bad... in the leg... shattered... Lost a lot of blood... I need your help to get her out... they won't let me through.

COSTA
Fuck... I'll try to find someone...

TERESA
Got to be you!... Please!... The road to the hospital is blocked... police won't let anyone through.

A tense Sebastián looks at Costa, who stares back at him.

COSTA
I can't Teresa... we're just about to pull out... I'll send down a car... [Looking at her desperate face] What can I do?!

TERESA
...If she's with a foreigner they might let her through... we're using the post office for the wounded...

COSTA
Shit...

TERESA
Help me, please... You got Daniel out of jail... you can do it...

He glances at the nervous crew and then Sebastián.

COSTA
[To Teresa] Wait here.

Costa takes a few steps away. Sebastián follows him.

COSTA (CONT'D)
Fuck! Fuck!

The crew are stunned.

COSTA (CONT'D)
I've got to go...

SEBASTIAN
[Exploding] No fucking way Costa! It's a war zone... [pointing at the radio]... you'll get yourself killed! There's nothing you can do! Tell her the truth! You are not going! We need you here!

Costa hesitates as he stares at all the faces now looking at him.

COSTA
[Going up to Teresa again] I'm sorry Teresa... I can't do it! I'm responsible for my entire crew! I can't leave them now!

TERESA
She could die... help me...

COSTA
Fuck... I'm sorry Teresa... [Moving away from her; to the crew] Come on! Let's get the hell out of here!

Costa and Sebastián look at each other for a second as everyone starts piling into the vehicles. Costa shuts the door of the minivan with the actors.

TERESA
She's my only girl.

Teresa looks at him for one last moment and then heads off, broken hearted. It's too much for Costa. He calls out to her.

COSTA
Teresa!

Costa turns to Sebastián who is getting into his 4 x 4.

COSTA (CONT'D)
I'm going to take Belen to the hospital... I'll catch up with you later! Promise. I'll catch up. Now get a move on! Out of here!

Sebastián grabs his arm.

> SEBASTIAN
> You can't go Costa... I need you...
>
> COSTA
> If something happens to that girl... I can't live with that... I've got to go...
>
> SEBASTIAN
> [Quietly, but determined] A thousand battles all over the world every day!... All heroic... all tragic... I'm a selfish bastard... [with great conviction] long after this dispute is done and forgotten our film will last... We can't fight with rocks... we fight with this [tapping his head]... our ideas... imagination...
>
> COSTA
> She's just twelve!
>
> SEBASTIAN
> You could get killed!

Costa looks at Teresa, who's waiting.

> COSTA
> She could die Sebastián...
>
> SEBASTIAN
> And what can you do?
>
> COSTA
> Don't know... but I've got to try.

Costa brushes Sebastián aside, climbs into his 4 x 4 with Teresa, and drives off. Sebastián watches him head away into the distance. Concerned looks on the faces of the actors as they stare at Sebastián.

## 49. MISCELLANEOUS ROADS OUTSIDE COCHABAMBA – DAY

Costa speeds back towards Cochabamba as Teresa points the way. They pass by a group of Indians who try to wave him down but he speeds on. Teresa points him to a side road, to avoid the roadblocks. The 4 x 4 spins off the main road and hammers across a dry riverbed as Teresa clings on to her seat.

## 50. EXT/ INT.CONVOY, MAIN ROAD – AFTERNOON

The film crew are in convoy along the highway. A glum-faced Sebastián and other actors are in the minivan. Sebastián tunes in to a radio station and they listen with alarm to the breathy voice of an eye witness to the battle.

> RADIO COMMENTATOR
> …I'm at the corner!… I can see the Water HQ! One block away… I can see the flagpole! Soldiers are crouched down behind a solid wall of sandbags… they are armed with guns… tear gas… rubber bullets… behind me is a most incredible sight… students, irrigantes, campesinos, and now cocaleros are lining up behind… My God… I think they're going to charge!… There must be around two thousand people here… more are streaming in from the side streets! More women carrying rocks… here they go… a raggle taggle army!

The commentator's voice is drowned out by the charge, shouts and explosions.

Sebastián looks pale. Maria touches his arm in support. Sebastián tries to make a call on his mobile. No coverage.

He listens in to more explosions and sounds of battle.

## 51. EXT/INT 4 X 4 ROADS OUTSIDE COCHABAMBA – DAY

Costa speeds along alternative tracks; he gets to an asphalted street, where he sees some two dozen Indians blocking their way with huge stones. Others dig holes. They signal to him to stop. He does so. Teresa speaks in Quechua to one of the leaders who is wearing a mask. The Indians let them through. The car speeds away.

## 52. INT./EXT. CONVOY, PETROL STATION – DAY

Sebastián and crew are glued to the radio as the convoy advances slowly. The strain tells. They can hear rifle fire and human screams.

> **CREW 1**
> Live fucking ammo… Snipers!

Shouts of concern all round.

> **MARIA**
> There'll be a massacre!

> **RADIO COMMENTATOR**
> The army are firing live ammo!… I've seen a dozen drop… but still they charge! Rocks against bullets… bodies falling all around me… dozens of injured people… cocaleros hurl Molotovs and dynamite charges at the soldiers… Another man down… they don't seem to care… more replace the fallen…

An explosion and the voices go dead; radio silence. Sebastián can take it no more. He switches off the radio. He grabs his mobile again, and makes another attempt to call.

> **SEBASTIAN**
> Fucking hell Costa, answer!

> **MARIA**
> He'll be okay… I know he will.

AHEAD: A military checkpoint, by a petrol station.

Soldiers stop every vehicle. They spot several army trucks, manned by tough-faced soldiers who look like they mean business and await orders.

ALBERTO
Where the fuck is our great producer when we need him?

SEBASTIAN
[In a fit of fury] Risking his fucking life!

53. EXT. COCHABAMBA STREETS – EVENING

Costa driving as fast as he can, following Teresa's directions. He passes ever larger groups of people of all ages, from city and country alike, at street corners, armed with sticks and stones, many of whom have bandannas over their faces.

A group prepare Molotovs.

In the distance, the sound of gunfire; a helicopter hovers overhead. He turns a corner sharply and speeds down a street.

Another corner: A quite incredible sight, almost medieval. Costa stares in awe: a long line of Indian women, their shawls filled with rocks, deposit their heavy loads in a corner. Young men, wearing bandannas, and faces streaked with bicarbonate of soda, rush for more 'ammunition'.

Other youngsters prepare sling-shots. At another corner, a medic treats more wounded for burns and cuts. Others, exhausted, lean up against a wall to rest.

54. EXT. SIDE OF THE ROAD, SERVICE STATION – AFTERNOON

The convoy gradually slows down, till it practically comes to a halt. A soldier instructs them to stop on the side of the road. The minivan with more crew pulls up behind them.

Distant sound of gunfire that makes them even more uneasy. Three trucks full of soldiers thunder into the service station.

One truck pulls up near them. A van pulls out in front of them to give them a clear view of the soldiers in the truck ahead. Several soldiers on the back kick down the tailgate of the truck to jump down. The crew are stunned. Some eighteen Indians are lying face down, with hands tied behind their backs. Most are still. One tries to lift his head.

A young, teenaged soldier goes berserk and pounds the man on the neck with the butt of his rifle.

Maria screams in shock.

### ALBERTO
He just broke his neck!

They are all shaken by the brutality.

### JUAN
Is he dead?… What about the others?

The soldier stares at them threateningly and snaps the tailgate up.

### SEBASTIAN
Stop looking at him for Christ's sake!

The soldier rushes round to the other side of the truck and yells at the driver to leave. They head off to the other side of the service station parking area.

Juan, Alberto, and Maria stare at each other. They catch sight of other members of the crew, shocked, in another minivan beside them. They also witnessed the brutality. They roll down the windows to talk to each other.

### CREW 1
Fuck this… we're going straight to the airport!
That's enough.

### CREW 2
Let's go! Now!

### ALBERTO
[To Juan] We're out of here… That's it!

Juan hesitates as he looks at Sebastián.

                    JUAN
          Come on! Let's go… all of us… you too
          Sebastián… this is a fucking nightmare… I've got
          a family, waiting for me…

Maria hugs Sebastián with great affection.

                    MARIA
          I'm so sorry Sebastián… This is too much for
          me…

She kisses his cheek and takes her bag.

                    MARIA (CONT'D)
          You should come too…

                    ALBERTO
          Anton?

He glances at Sebastián.

                    ANTON
          I've got no one waiting for me…

Juan, Alberto and a reluctant Maria rush over to the other vehicle. Sebastián is too stunned to react or to argue with them; he just watches them go.

The driver of the minivan, after a brief conversation with a policeman, pulls out. Maria's distraught face at the open window watches Sebastián.

Sebastián feels dizzy and shattered. He steps outside, goes over to a little wall and just sits there. Anton, with a bottle of water in his hand, joins him, sitting down beside him.

                    ANTON (CONT'D)
          I'm sorry Sebastián…

Sebastián stares at the chaos around him; then at the young soldiers on the back of other lorries.

                    SEBASTIAN
          It's over…

ANTON
You tried Sebastián… you took a chance… that's the point!

Sebastián shakes his head.

ANTON (CONT'D)
Courage of your conviction!… [pause] I never did… always been too scared…

SEBASTIAN
Bravest of all…

Anton shakes his head. Sebastián stares at him.

ANTON
You are still young… 'your own man'… the only thing I was ever good at was pretending to be someone else…

SEBASTIAN
Best actor I've ever seen…

ANTON
So what? [Pause] I'm a useless father… a pathetic prick all round. Wish I had my time again.

In the truck closest to them young soldiers order several Indians to get off. One, badly beaten, with blood on his face, falls as he tries to scramble down. He struggles to get on his knees.

Anton walks towards him. The young soldier stares at him, tensely, and raises his rifle. Anton just ignores the young soldier, bends down, cradles the shoulder of the fallen man, and gives him some water from his bottle. The soldier, confused, just stands there looking at him with rifle in hand.

Sebastián just stares at them, then buries his face in his hands.

## 55. EXT/INT. 4 X 4, STREETS, COCHABAMBA POST OFFICE – DAY

Miscellaneous scenes of growing danger.

The 4 x 4 comes upon a dozen soldiers running towards them with dogs. Costa jams on the brakes and reverses at speed. In the mirror he sees that more soldiers have blocked his route. Screech of brakes.

### TERESA
Down that way!

He accelerates down a little lane. He is just about to swerve into that lane when he sees two soldiers drop to their knees and take aim. They swerve down a bumpy little road but only end up at a T-junction. Before them all they can see are flying rocks and the flash of tear gas.

### COSTA
Jesus Christ!

He swerves into the road and finds himself in no man's land in the middle of a full-blown riot. To one side are dozens of police in protective armour, firing rubber bullets and tear gas. A rubber bullet smashes his rear passenger window. On the other side are some one hundred and fifty Indians hurling rocks at the police.

Costa starts speeding towards the Indians. They are stunned to see a 4 x 4 rushing towards them.

Costa drives through the chaos and, following Teresa's directions, makes his way to a makeshift medical post.

Costa and Teresa rush into the post office and stare at injured bodies lying around all over, with several exhausted young nurses and medics doing their best to attend to them.

Teresa spots Belen in a corner, being attended by a student nurse. Teresa rushes over to Belen, who is lying prostrate. She seems asleep. There is a blanket over her leg soaked in blood.

COSTA (CONT'D)
Jesus! [To nurse] How is she?

NURSE
Getting worse... very weak...

COSTA
I've got a vehicle outside... let's get her to a hospital... and anyone else we can fit in...

NURSE
There are police lines all over... you can't get through...

COSTA
I'll bribe the bastards!... Always works.

She jumps up and rushes towards the medic in charge to give him the good news.

Costa leans over a pale-faced, fading Belen and touches her brow. Belen opens her eyes. Costa is almost overcome.

COSTA (CONT'D)
We'll get you out of here...

BELEN
Where's my father?

COSTA
On his way Belen... Don't worry...

BELEN
I can't feel my leg...

Costa takes her hand and spots her sling-shot in her skirt pocket.

COSTA
I'll bring him to you... promise.

Belen's eyes close again. The medics pick out several of the wounded, depending on the seriousness of their condition. Costa and Teresa each hold one corner of the stretcher on which Belen lies and head out towards Costa's vehicle.

## 56. INT. HOSPITAL WAITING ROOM – NIGHT

Costa and Teresa sit beside each other in a packed waiting room. Some try to grab a few moments' rest.

Costa opens his eyes as four men rush in carrying a wounded man covered in blood. They disappear behind the doors to the emergency ward and their shouts fade.

## 57. EXT. STREET OUTSIDE THE HOSPITAL – DAWN

Costa stands on the hospital steps and watches a group of fighters sprint towards the hospital pushing two wheelbarrows. The arms of the wounded men dangle from the improvised transport.

INSIDE THE WAITING ROOM: Costa sees an exhausted MEDIC open the swing doors. He spots Teresa and goes over towards her. Teresa gets up and after listening to him moves at speed towards the doors.

Costa turns to the doctor.

COSTA
How is she?

MEDIC
We got her… just in time. Lost a lot of blood… she's stable and should pull through…

COSTA
Thank Christ…

The medic's face darkens.

MEDIC
I hope we can save her leg… touch and go… time will tell.

Costa is stunned.

COSTA
I've got to find her father.

## 58. EXT. STREETS IN COCHABAMBA – EARLY MORNING

Costa drives down an abandoned street covered in rubble. There is the sound of shots, but far off in the distance. He reaches a corner and hesitates. He looks down a short street and is stunned to see the Water HQ at the end facing them. It is eerily silent and abandoned. The wall of sandbags has been toppled and a way through has been opened to the Water Building.

The water company flag has been pulled down and instead flies a Bolivian flag.

The street is so covered with rocks, cartridges, barricades, and corrugated metal that the vehicle can't pass. Costa gets out of his vehicle and stares at the aftermath of the battle. He spots an Indian staring down at him from a third-storey window.

> COSTA
> Where's the army?

The man just stares at him.

Costa walks towards the Water Building. He steps over rocks and patches of blood and then in the distance he hears a sound. He stops. The peals of a remarkable bell. It grows stronger.

Then he spots a dreamlike image move towards him. A PRIEST, in a long black soutane, rings the bell and shouts out to his invisible audience.

> PRIEST
> No more fighting... No more fighting... the army have been ordered to pull out and the water company is leaving the country... The water is ours!... The water is ours!

The priest turns down a different street as his bell and repeated message grows dimmer.

Costa walks closer to the Water Building. He stands there alone for a few quiet moments contemplating the devastation around him.

## 59. INT. WAREHOUSE – DAY

Costa, in fresh clothes, slips off his packed rucksack and lays it on the ground. He wanders around the abandoned film warehouse in complete silence.

The place is a mess with miscellaneous materials. He picks up bits and pieces and lays them down again. His phone rings, and he answers. [He continues to wander as he talks.]

> COSTA
> Where are you?

> SEBASTIAN
> At the airport... the rest have gone. How's Belen?

> COSTA
> She'll pull through...

> SEBASTIAN
> Thank God... and you... are you okay?

Long pause.

> COSTA
> Could be worse... Columbus went back in chains...

> SEBASTIAN
> [Chuckles] I'm not giving up Costa... not even now.

> COSTA
> You never do... [looking around at the mess] 'The film comes first'.

> SEBASTIAN
> Yeah... I'm a bastard. I'll wait for you here.

> COSTA
> You don't have to Sebastián...

> SEBASTIAN
> Yes I do.

The phone goes dead.

Costa passes by some benches in the art department. His eyes flick though various crumpled-up and discarded sketches, at least one of the huge cross and others from Bartolomé de las Casas' infamous book.

Costa spots a bashed-up copy of half the script among debris and fishes it out. He examines it for a moment.

Costa hears footsteps and looks up. He sees Daniel walk towards him.

Daniel joins him. A moment between them.

                    COSTA
    How's Belen?

Daniel has to fight to control himself. He pulls something from his jacket and holds Belen's sling-shot. He fingers the rough cord and scuffed leather which looks like the tongue of an old shoe.

                    DANIEL
    She wanted to be with her brothers…

                    COSTA
    Her leg?

                    DANIEL
    We don't know yet…

After a few moments Costa puts his hand into his pocket and takes out a copy of the front page from an English-speaking newspaper he's pulled off the net. He unfolds it and hands it to Daniel.

                    COSTA
    Big news…

Daniel stares at a dramatic photograph of celebrating rioters outside the Water HQ. An adolescent pulls down the corporate flag as friends below shout in delight. Headline reads: 'Multinational flees Bolivia after Water War'.

Costa points to a figure with a loudspeaker in the photograph.

> COSTA (CONT'D)
> That's you.

Daniel stares for some moments.

> DANIEL
> Always costs us dear… every time. Wish there was another way… [Pause] Now for the tough bit… make the water supply work for everybody… won't be easy… [Pause] What are you going to do now?

> COSTA
> I don't know… [Glancing at the script] Help Sebastián finish this… if we can… God knows how…

> DANIEL
> Your friend's a fighter… I admire that…

Costa stares at him for a few moments.

> COSTA
> What are you going to do Daniel?

> DANIEL
> Survive… that's what we do.

Costa nods. He glances at the script in his hand and throws it onto the bench.

> COSTA
> I'm going to help you with Belen… a promise.

Daniel nods quietly.

In the distance a taxi pulls up in front of the warehouse and pumps its horn.

> DANIEL
> [Mischievous glint, awkward English] And the old trucks you were going to leave behind? Where are they?

Costa shakes his head in shame.

                              COSTA
    Ben Hur...

Daniel chuckles.

                              DANIEL
    El Cid...

They hold each other's eye.

                         DANIEL (CONT'D)
    Will we see you again?

                              COSTA
    I don't think so...

                              DANIEL
    I brought you a little present...

Daniel hands him a tidy little box wrapped up carefully.

                              COSTA
    Thank you...

                              DANIEL
    You saved my daughter's life... you know that.

Costa drops his head and fights back the tears.

They embrace warmly for a long moment.

Costa grabs his rucksack and heads towards the taxi. They watch each other disappear.

### 60. EXT. COCHABAMBA STREETS – DAY

As the taxi drives through the now familiar streets of Cochabamba – with many parts still bearing the scars of the riot – Costa stares down at the wrapped-up box in front of him.

He glances back at the streets, metal sheeting and piles of rocks swept up to corners.

Street kids beg at traffic lights, but the taxi is gone and through them before Costa can react.

The burnt-out bodies of buses and cars still pepper the landscape. Costa looks down at the box and hesitates before opening it up. He unfurls the string and cracks the box open.

Lying inside, wrapped up in straw, as if it were precious wine, is a bottle of clear bright liquid with a carefully sealed cork. Costa carefully takes it out and holds it up to the light.

He smiles to himself.

The taxi driver catches Costa's face in the mirror.

> COSTA
> [In Quechua] Yaku [Water].

OUT IN THE STREET:

Costa's taxi passes through a gang of kids playing football among the rocks and battered sheets of metal. They run, shout, tackle and are totally lost in the moment.

FADE TO BLACK:

Verse of Arawak song with the following subtitles:

> INDIAN VOICE
> 'We were happy when he first came, we thought he came from the light. But he comes like the dusk of the evening now, not like the dawn of morning. He comes like a day that was passed and night enters our future with him.'

# Cast and Crew

*CAST*

| | |
|---|---|
| Costa | Luis Tosar |
| Sebastián | Gael García Bernal |
| Daniel/Hatuey | Juan Carlos Aduviri |
| Anton/Christopher Columbus | Karra Elejalde |
| Alberto/Bartolomé de las Casas | Carlos Santos |
| Juan/Antonio de Montesinos | Raúl Arévalo |

*CREW*

| | |
|---|---|
| Director | Icíar Bollaín |
| Producer | Juan Gordon |
| Produced by | Morena Films (Spain) |
| Co-produced by | Mandarin Cinema (France) |
| | Alebrije Cine y Video (Mexico) |
| | Vaca Films (Spain) |
| Screenplay | Paul Laverty |
| Line Producer | Cristina Zumárraga |
| Production Designer | Juan Pedro de Gaspar |
| Director of Photography | Alex Catalán |
| Editor | Ángel Hernández Zoido |
| Sound | Emilio Cortés |
| Music | Alberto Iglesias |
| Make-up | Karmele Soler |
| Hairstylist | Paco Rodríguez |
| Costume Designer | Sonia Grande |
| Casting | Eva Leira and Yolanda Serrano (Spain) |
| | Rodrigo Bellot and Glenda Rodríguez (Bolivia) |

## PAUL LAVERTY

A Palme d'Or and nine films written by him and directed by Ken Loach have won Paul Laverty recognition as an acclaimed scriptwriter. Born in Calcutta, his concern for social issues led him to work for a human rights organisation in Nicaragua. His experiences in Central America took him away from his work as a lawyer in Scotland and inspired him to write the script for *Carla's Song*, his first film with Loach.

*Carla's Song* was to be the beginning of one of the most prolific professional relationships in contemporary cinema and was followed by, among others, *My Name is Joe*, *Bread and Roses*, *Sweet Sixteen* (Best Screenplay at Cannes 2002), *The Wind That Shakes the Barley* (Palme d'Or, Cannes 2006), *It's a Free World* (Best screenplay award in Venice), *Looking for Eric* and, most recently, *Route Irish*.

## ICIAR BOLLAIN

Icíar Bollaín was born in Madrid in 1967. Her interest in cinema can be traced back to her teenage years and her roles in films such as Victor Erice's *El Sur* (*The South*) and Manuel Gutierrez Aragon's *Malaventura* (*Misadventure*). She subsequently appeared in *Tocando Fondo*, directed by José Luis Cuerda, *Tierra y Libertad* (*Land and Freedom*), by Ken Loach, and Jose Luis Borau's *Niño Nadie* (1997) and *Leo* (2000), for which she was nominated for the Goya for Best Actress.

She made her debut as a director in 1995 with *¿Hola, estás sola?* (*Hi, Are You Alone?*) at the Valladolid Film Festival, where she won the Best New Director award. She subsequently directed *Flores de otro mundo* (*Flowers from Another World*) (1999), *Amores que matan* (2000) and *Te doy mis ojos* (*Take My Eyes*) (2003) – for which she won seven Goyas, including Best Director, Best Original Screenplay and Best Film. For *Mataharis*, the last film she has directed, she received two Goya nominations.

## *Looking For Eric*
Written by Paul Laverty, Directed by Ken Loach
ISBN: 978-1901927-41-2

Eric the postman is slipping through his own fingers... His chaotic family, his wild stepsons, and the cement mixer in the front garden don't help, but it is Eric's own secret that drives him to the brink. Can he face Lily, the woman he once loved thirty years ago? Despite outrageous efforts and misplaced goodwill from his football fan mates, Eric continues to sink.

In desperate times it takes a spliff and a special friend from foreign parts to challenge a lost postman to make that journey into the most perilous territory of all – the past. As the Chinese, and one Frenchman, say, 'He who is afraid to throw the dice, will never throw a six.'

Features the full screenplay, including extra scenes, sixteen pages of colour photographs, plus introductions from Paul Laverty, Ken Loach, Eric Cantona and production notes from the cast and crew.

## *Route Irish*
Written by Paul Laverty, Directed by Ken Loach
ISBN: 978-1901927-47-4

Fergus met Frankie on his first day at school and they've been in each other's shadow ever since. As teenagers they skipped school and drank cider on the ferry over the River Mersey, dreaming about travelling the world. In September 2004, Fergus persuaded Frankie to join his security team in Baghdad: £10,000 a month, tax free; their last chance to 'load up' in this increasingly privatised war. Together they risked their lives in a city steeped in violence, terror and greed, and awash with billions of US dollars. Three years later, Frankie is killed on Route Irish, the most dangerous road in the world.

Back in Liverpool, a grief-stricken Fergus rejects the official explanation that Frankie was simply in the wrong place at the wrong time, and begins his own investigation into his soul mate's death. Only Rachel, Frankie's partner, grasps the depth of Fergus's sorrow, and the lethal possibilities of his fury as he struggles to find his old self and the happiness he shared with Frankie twenty years earlier on the Mersey.

Features the full screenplay, character backstory, production notes and photographs from the film, plus background essays by Mark Townsend, Haifa Zangana and Mike Phipps.

For further information on these books,
and other titles from Route please visit:

**www.route-online.com**